A PROMISE
IS TO KEEP

D1468677

Profile portrait of Eliza, 1910
(Courtesy of the Maryland Historical Society)

A PROMISE IS TO KEEP

*The True Story of a Former Slave
and the Family She Adopted*

NAN HAYDEN AGLE

Zondervan Books
Zondervan Publishing House
Grand Rapids, Michigan

A Promise Is to Keep

Zondervan Books are published by the Zondervan Publishing House
1415 Lake Drive, S.E., Grand Rapids, Michigan 49506

Copyright © 1985 by Nan Hayden Agle
Grand Rapids, Michigan

Library of Congress Cataloging in Publication Data

Agle, Nan Hayden.
    A promise is to keep.

1. Benson, Eliza Ann. 2. Afro-Americans—Maryland—Biography. 3.
Slaves—Maryland—Biography. 4. Maryland—Biography. 5. Spencer
family. I. Title.
E185.97.B333A65   1985   975.2'00496073   85-22803
ISBN 0-310-41591-8

Edited by John D. Sloan
Designed by Carole Parrish

Printed in the United States of America

86   87   88   89   90 / 10   9   8   7   6   5

To Eliza herself
and my grandparents,
Miss Braddie and Marse Edward

Contents

Acknowledgments

Prologue

1 Different Kinds of Sorrow   13

2 A Promise   18

3 The Beginning   24

4 Good Times   29

5 The Deep Dip   35

6 Miss Braddie   41

7 The Accident   47

8 Mount Pleasant   53

9 Putting Down New Roots   60

10 Miss Em's Cousin Edward   69

11 School Days, One Kind and Another   74

12 The First Blue Letter   83

13 A Few Visits and a Whole Lot of Letters   89

14 At the Bottom of the Well   100

15 At The Martin's Nest   104

16 People and Politics   113

17 Shiny Bright Needle   118

18 Heart Break   124

19 Eliza Makes a Speech   135

20 Mrs. Smyth's Boarding House   143

21 Next to Last Era   152

Epilogue   158

Acknowledgments

Thanks to:

> *John Agle, my husband*
> *Gellert Spencer Alleman, my cousin Bill, and his wife, Anita*
> *Ruth Hayden Wanzer, my sister*
> *Ridgely and Shirley Cecil, my son and my daughter-in-law*
> *Polly Spencer, Cousin Lindsly's wife*
> *Mr. and Mrs. Harold F. Hutchinson of "Clay's Hope"*
> *Barbara Moody at the Enoch Pratt Free Library*
> *And Eleanor Merryman Roszel Rogers, my friend and agent*

The photographs of Eliza were taken by my mother Emily Spencer Hayden, a member of the small group of early 1900 Baltimore photographers. Permission to print the photographs in *A Promise Is to Keep* was graciously granted by Laurie Baty, former Prints and Photographs Librarian at The Maryland Historical Society, and Jay M. Fisher, Associate Curator of Prints, Drawings, and Photographs at the Baltimore Museum of Art.

Prologue

That Eliza was born a slave is beside the point. Small in body and monumental in character, she was a "Worthy of Maryland" for three generations.

As the least member of the third generation, I was fortunate to hear Eliza tell her story in her own way, using her own words. I was fortunate to hear about Rosa, Mable, Tom, Marse Bradford, and most important Miss Braddie and Master Edward, my grandparents.

During her long and valuable life, Eliza rose "above tribulation" and stayed there until she went to glory.

1

Different Kinds of Sorrow

On a sunny day in June when Eliza was almost eighty years old and I was ten, the two of us were in the big, old kitchen at "Nancy's Fancy," our home in Catonsville. She was standing beside the long wooden table sifting flour into a yellow mixing bowl, and I was close by sitting on the bottom step of the backstairs, hot tears rolling down my plump cheeks.

"You ought to be ashamed of yourself, Miss Nan, bellerin' like Tyson's Bull over nothin' more than missin' a Sunday School picnic," Eliza said without looking up.

To be scolded by her instead of being comforted was too much to bear. I sobbed, explaining between sobs, "It's not an ordinary picnic. This year it's at Bay Shore. Right now practically everybody I know except Daddy and Grandma is on the streetcar going there. And not an ordinary streetcar either—an open car with sideways seats."

Since Eliza didn't seem to be impressed I added, "Everybody's singing and having a great time, and here I sit. The back platform full of buckets of fried chicken, boxes of sandwiches, cakes, freezers of ice cream, and frozen custard. I adore frozen custard!"

Eliza was still not moved, so I added in a doleful tone, "And scads of deviled eggs." I didn't use the word "scads" often. It was a college word borrowed from my sister Ruth by my sister Catherine and me to use on special occasions. Ruth was seven years older than Catherine, and I was three years younger than Catherine—almost three years.

Eliza—short, rounded, small-boned, and cinnamon brown—crossed the wide kitchen floor, her full skirts swinging. She always wore at least two skirts, no telling how many petticoats, a long-sleeved neat shirt with a small white collar close to the neck, and a white head handkerchief.

I watched her bend down, open the lower half of the double door of the cupboard next to the iron stove, and take out two bread pans, black from many bakings. Straightening up, she glanced at me. I must have looked pitiful, for she pulled a large, man-sized, snow-white handkerchief out of a hidden pocket in the top skirt, handed it to me, and said, "Blow your nose, chile."

I blew a loud, unladylike snort and then said, "Last year's picnic was at Primrose Farm. Remember?"

"Deed I do," Eliza answered, nodding her round head. "I recollect you saw a fox."

"Two foxes," I told her as she began the mystical ritual of making bread. Oh, her bread was wonderful. Just to smell it was enough to make you swoon. "Young foxes they were with red coats and pretty red tails tipped in white. They were playing like puppies around the rocky entrance to their den. I wouldn't have missed seeing them for anything. First time ever to see wild, free foxes close up."

Eliza nodded her head again, enjoying the foxes through me. She was great at enjoying things both firsthand and through us. I enjoyed things firsthand best, except for things through Eliza. But right then I was too unhappy to enjoy anything. With a sigh I said, "Last year's picnic was so good. This year's is going to be much better, I just know it is, and I'm missing it."

After a long silence during which the clock ticked its loudest, I said to Eliza, "This year there will be swimming in the bay, as long as you want to swim, and riding on the merry-go-round, free for as many rides as you want. Of all the things in the world to do, riding on a merry-go-round is the most fun; and next to that is swimming in the bay." Eliza said she'd take my word for it.

Anger swept over me. I banged the kitchen floor with my heels saying, "I am *so* well enough to go! I've been out of bed two whole days, no fever at all, and the only chicken pox scab left anywhere is a small one on my belly."

"Never mind mentionin' your parts," Eliza said firmly.

Pretending not to hear the reproof, I flung out my arms dramatically. "Beautiful day, beautiful green lawn, beautiful trees, spring, stream, house, barn, porches, attic, beautiful animals, beautiful everything; and it all adds up to nothing when you are sad as I am." Looking at the kitchen clock on the mantel over the stove, I remarked, "Eleven-fifteen. They are there by now, everybody racing to do whatever they are going to do, and here I sit full of sorrow."

A Promise is to Keep

"You don't know what sorrow is, Miss Nan," Eliza told me. She leaned across the table, lifted down the square wooden salt box from the shelf, and measured salt in the pale palm of her wrinkled hand. "When your mother was your age, she knew. Poor Miss Em'ly. Your Aunt Katharine, jes' six years old she was den, she knew, an' so did your Uncle Robbie an' Uncle Lindsly, half-grown boys back then. They knew what sorrow was."

"Why did they? What made them know and me not know?" I asked, frowning, feeling left out of deep living, deprived of full measure.

"Their mother died," Eliza said. "Broke my heart, dat day did. Miss Braddie was too young to die. She didn't want to leave her children an' Marse Edward behind, dem needin' her so. Like I tell you, Miss Nan, you don't know what sorrow is."

"Yes I do," I answered sharply in my own defense. "I've buried dead birds, dead rabbits, dead butterflies, dead bugs. One black beetle I buried was shiny and perfect with beautifully shaped feet that had branches on them. Not toes, Eliza—branches. Seeing those tiny branches, you knew he was kin to trees and plants as well as to other bugs and us. I hated to bury him in the ground. I hate death, hate it, hate it! Being dead is not to see or hear or feel or know. It is never to go to a picnic or have any fun at all, anyplace, ever."

"Not a bit a use you goin' on 'bout death. He don't listen to nobody. Poor Miss Braddie," Eliza said as she went through the dining room to the pantry.

I heard the pantry door shut behind her, and right away I heard music inside my head—merry-go-round music: "In the good old summer time, in the good old

16

summer time ..." The picnickers were really hearing it, the merry-go-round was going around and around, mirror lights flashing as the music played.

"Eliza," I said when she came back into the kitchen with the butter that she had brought to soften, "I'm hungry."

"I reckon so. Haven't had a blessed thing to eat since breakfast, have ya?"

She went back to the pantry and returned with a piece of fried chicken on a saucer, left over from the night before. It was a second joint, my favorite piece.

"There you are," she said.

I bit into the chicken with mixed feelings, feelings of lust and feelings of hope that the meat was not part of one of our own, known to me since an egg—intimately known. I wished things did not have double edges. Eliza didn't. She was the same always, rock-solid yesterday, today, and tomorrow.

I felt sorry for all of the children in the world who did not have Eliza, who set aside special things for them to eat when they couldn't go to picnics; Eliza, who kept things special as well as promises special until her dying day.

2

A Promise

Still sitting on the bottom step of the stairs, I watched Eliza expertly handle the bread dough. I watched her shape it in her hands, lay it in the yellow bowl, cover the bowl with a clean tea towel, and push it back against the wall out of the way. I watched her wash her hands at the sink as she had done a million times before, dry them on the roller towel on the back door, then sit down in her chair under the window. Hands folded in her lap, head bent down, she rested.

Silence filled the whole house except for the tictoc of the kitchen clock, its toc much deeper than its tic. Outdoors wasn't silent. Mr. Kreger was cutting the lawn, and of all the sounds to make you feel lonely when everybody else was at a picnic, the lawn mower was in first place. Even with Eliza right there, I felt lonely and guilty too. Eliza should have been enough, but when you are ten years old nothing is enough. I seethed with unnameable wants.

A hen set up a great cackling down at the barn and I said, "Another egg, Eliza."

She nodded her head. The lonely tictoc sound and

A Promise

the shrill noise of a distant bug pointed up how quiet
the rest of the world was except for the lawn mower.

After a while Eliza said, "Dis mebbe my last summer
on dis earth."

I wished she hadn't said it. Missing the picnic,
hearing about my grandmother's death, and remembering the sadness that brought to all the children was
enough. She'd said things like that before: her last
Christmas, her last Thanksgiving, her last Easter. One
last really would be the last. I shook my head to get rid
of the thought, and Eliza said, "I want you chillen to see
to it Mr. Charley don't bury me in de colored graveyard
where de body snatcher kin get me. The onlies' place I
kin rest is next to Miss Braddie in de fam'ly graveyard."

"Of course you'll be there, Eliza," I told her. "You
are a member of the family."

She got to her feet. Rubbing the small of her back
with her hands, she said, "I know dat, Miss Nan. You
know it. Miss Cathern and Miss Ruth an' Miss Em'ly
know it. What Mr. Charley know is another kettle a
fish."

My father never needed any defending. His slate was
as clean as a hound's dinner plate. His character was as
straight as the pine tree on the lawn. Nevertheless, I
said, "Daddy always does the right thing."

"Mebbe he do an' mebbe he don't. He a Yankee;
him, Grandma Hayden, an' Auntie—all three Yankees.
No tellin' what dey think or do, Miss Nan. You can't
predick what a foreigner got on his mind."

"My father is not a foreigner, Eliza. He is as
American as we are."

"To be on de safe side, I want ya to promise me here
an' now you'll see to it I am laid to res' where I tell ya,
close to Miss Braddie."

19

A Promise is to Keep

"I promise."

She was right: to make a promise is serious and not to be taken lightly. The burden of the promise just made rested heavily on my shoulders.

Looking out the window, her back to me, Eliza said, "I mus' be close to Miss Braddie on Judgment Day. She wouldn't go on to glory widout me an' she wouldn't want to keep Marse Edward waitin' whilst she hunt all over Kingdom Come fer me. I mus' be right dere on han'."

A vision of Judgment Day landed on me. I saw clearly a long line of saints dressed in white trailing off toward a huge pink cloud in the west that I presumed was "glory."

Eliza chuckled, and the vision vanished.

"What's funny?" I asked, wondering how anything could be humorous with all this talk about death, burial, and a promise to keep.

"Miss Braddie funny, dat's what," Eliza said, turning toward me, laugh wrinkles showing around her eyes, her mouth turning up at the corners. "Put all de sorrow in de world in a lump an' Miss Braddie would balance it out. Always singin', dancin', havin' fun, her black eyes shinin' like hot fat, an' her long, straight, black hair shiny as a mare's tail on Sunday."

"But you said she died and broke your heart," I said standing up, flinging my arms wide. "You said my grandmother died and left four full-of-sorrow children and a husband who could not get along without her."

"She did. She did. February 27, 1882, it was. I'd died in her place a hundred times over if de Good Lord would a let me. Wasn't I hers? Wasn't I given to her when she was practically bran' new? Me, four years old, given outright to her as a gift by Marse Bradford himself."

"Who was he?"

"Marse Bradford Harrison, Miss Braddie's father, your great grandfather, dat's who. De finess man ever walked on dis earth. He gave me to her."

"You can't give people," I said in astonishment.

"Not now, you can't. Back then, if you a slave you could be home Monday an' gone de next day, sold an' gone, your Sunday coat still hangin' on de peg behind de door waitin' for somebody else to wear it to church. Not many got demselves given as a gift, though. Not any I ever hear' tell of 'cept me."

I sat down in Mr. Kreger's chair. He ate at a table of his own over under the side window, not at Eliza's table. He was white and a cut below her—two or three cuts actually. But Eliza herself was not perfect. She had one flaw: vanity. Her own brand of vanity, such as refusing to eat with Mr. Kreger because he picked his teeth and used hair oil. And he belched. When he'd belch, which he nearly always did after supper, Eliza would say under her breath: "Buzzard."

My thoughts went back to slavery.

"Sold or given, it's dreadful," I said indignantly. "Slavery was terrible and if there is any of it left anywhere, it still is terrible."

Eliza sat down in the spare chair at Mr. Kreger's table beside me, since we could still hear the lawn mower. Elbow resting on the table, chin resting in her hand, she said, "To some it was. Anybody who had *Uncle Tom's Cabin* read to dem know dat. I had it read to me three times, Miss Nan, by Miss Braddie, Miss Em'ly your mother, an' then again later on by Miss Ruth. Poor

21

Tom, taken away from his wife an' chile, sold to a cruel master. Terrible like you say, Miss Nan." She thought a moment before adding, "Even so, a body know you can't open de barnyard gate an' speck to have a blade a grass lef' standing on de lawn. Marse Bradford ease his slaves out when dey ready to go, when dey thirty-one year old an' worth somepin' to demselves."

"What do you mean, ease them out?" I asked, frowning and scratching that last chicken pox bump.

Eliza leaned back comfortably in the chair. By the contented expression on her old face, I guessed she was thinking about long ago. She was. "Marse Bradford took care of his people. He saw to it everybody had a roof, a fire, plenty to eat, an' work to do. Time he set dem free when dey thirty-one an' know how to take care of demselves, he say come back if dey sick or when dey old, come on back home. An' he give dem a mule to ride off on."

"Did you get free when you were thirty-one, Eliza?"

"I would have, same as de res', if Mr. Lincoln hadn't freed everybody already."

"Abraham Lincoln, President Lincoln?"

"That's him. Miss Braddie tell me he didn't set out to. He dead set on keeping de country together, an' he had to free de slaves or lose out. Country laid bare by war, nothin' planted in de ground 'cept a million young men, an' he turn all my people out a house an' home, to root hog or die."

Feeling very learned. I said, "The Emancipation Proclamation, January ·1, 1863, is next to the most important document anywhere. Well, maybe not second. The Declaration of Independence, Constitution, Bill of Rights, and it are all important." Before, things like that had been history in books. Now Eliza made them real.

"What did you do on Emancipation Day?" I asked her.

She chuckled, covering her mouth with her hand so the smile wouldn't show. "Same as de day befo' an' de day after. I cook an' serve breakfast, lunch an' supper fer Miss Braddie, Marse Edward, an' his mother, ol' Miss Spencer. Miss Braddie married by then an' we livin' at 'The Martin's Nest' in Randallstown, de four of us, her, him, ol' Miss, and me."

I was disappointed in her answer and showed it. "I would have done something to celebrate if I'd been you—free for the first time ever."

"Freedom work both ways, chile. I was free to go an' free to stay. By dat time, wild horses couldn't pull me away from Miss Braddie. We'd been through de rip-raps together, her an' me. We boun' together fer always in a way words can't tell. You'd have to live out de whole story wid us to know how it was."

"Yes," I said, heading for the rope swing on the back porch. "The whole story." The thought went deep. Swinging low so I could think, I knew I wanted more than anything in the world to dig out all of the pieces of Eliza's life and fit them together. She was happy beyond sorrow—real sorrow, not Sunday School Picnic sorrow. That was bad enough. Happy and sure. There was no doubt in her. None.

What made her so sure, so happy?

Years went by before the pieces of Eliza's life began to fit together. The beginning was told to her by Mable, her mother, and Rosa, Mable's closest friend, in their own words; it was retold to me by Eliza in her own words.

3

The Beginning

It was Christmas Eve, 1836, cold and clear in Talbot County on the Eastern Shore of Maryland. Lamps in the dwelling house at Clay's Hope had been blown out. Mr. Bradford Harrison and his family had retired for the night: Marse Bradford himself (as he was called) and his wife Eleanor, side by side in the four poster in the front room. Down the hall in the room on the right the teen-age daughters Mary and Emily whispered about what might be in packages under the tree in the sitting room. The sons Samuel Alexander and Jonathan, home from college for the holidays, slept soundly in the back room.

In the stable the horses rested quietly. Sheep huddled close together in their shelter by the pasture gate. In the barn the cows lay in their stalls, all quiet, resting. Chickens slept in rows along roosts in the chicken house, and in the shed under the oak tree the turkeys slept.

Around three sides of the two-hundred-acre farm flowed Tarr Creek, the reflection of the Christmas Star shimmering on its mirror surface.

The Beginning

Between the water and the dwelling house stood the quarters, six two-story brick houses where the slaves of Clay's Hope lived. Wisps of smoke drifted up from brick chimneys and trailed off into the darkness.

A candle was burning in the second house where Tom Benson lived. Tom was Marse Bradford's favorite slave, and Tom's wife, big, strong Mable, was one of the Harrisons' most valuable possessions. Marse Bradford bought her seven years before from his friend William Townsend, the owner of the adjoining farm.

Tom and Mable had fallen in love in spite of the fence between the Harrison and Townsend properties. Tom told Marse Bradford who then bought Mable, brought her over on their side of the fence, and went to the wedding. Yes, Tom and Mable were married same as anybody else in Christ Episcopal Church, St. Michael's, by The Reverend Joseph Spencer. Reverend Spencer was close kin of Marse Bradford's wife, who was Miss Eleanor Spencer before her marriage.

Everybody agreed that Mable was a handsome bride. Dressed in white, a bouquet of daisies in her hand, she held her head high. Standing in front of the altar or anywhere else, she made two of Tom. He was slightly built and short, but a big, strong man nonetheless, big in mind and strong in character.

The marriage was happy and productive. By 1836 there were five children in the Benson family: Viney, Jonas, Marnie, Lilly, and Jake. That Christmas Eve all five were asleep on the second floor, Viney, Marnie, and Lilly in the big bed, the two boys in the small bed at the head of the steps.

Mable was too restless to sleep. She sat in her chair in front of the fire waiting for her sixth child to be born.

A Promise is to Keep

Tom, nervous over the imminent event, stirred the fire, sparks flying up, flames leaping red. He was silent, knowing Mable wanted him to be. She was silent too, waiting. After a while she said, "It time, Tom," and he took off out the door, running to the last house in the row as though dogs were after him.

Presently two forms hurried back to the house, Tom and Rock-of-Ages Rosa. Once the door was shut behind them to keep out the cold night air, Rosa said to Tom, "I hear little Jake stirrin' an' frettin'. Take him to my house an' keep him dere 'til de new baby come. Birthin' is fer wimmin. Jonas, he so soun' asleep he never bat an eye 'til sunup. Leave him be an' take de little one."

"Yes ma'am, Miss Rosa," Tom said, and in no time he was leaving the house with the sleepy boy in his arms, glad to go. He didn't want to hear his Mable moaning, which she was bound to do with birthing being the way it was.

As soon as the door closed behind them, Rosa brewed a pot of strong tea and handed a cupful to Mable saying, "Drink it hot as you can stand. It hep bring de baby an' ease its comin'. Don't be fearful. Rosa right here an' she know what to do."

Mable was not fearful. Hadn't she brought forth five and never lost a single one? She could have managed by herself if need be. Still, gripping Rosa's hand was comforting.

Just before midnight Eliza Ann Benson was born.

The next morning in the kitchen just off the dwelling house, Rosa was frying rabbit, two skillets over the fire at once. Hominy was cooking on the back of the stove, and apples and biscuits in the oven. Christmas breakfast

26

at Clay's Hope was always fried rabbit, hominy, apples, biscuits and gravy. Plenty for everybody in the house and in the kitchen.

The door opened and in came Henry with an armful of chunk wood. "Merry Christmas," he said, dumping the wood in the almost-empty wood box by the stove. "Mmmmmm, somepin' smell good."

Rosa turned a rabbit leg with a long tined fork. "It is a Merry Christmas fer fair. Mable baby born las' night, a girl name Eliza."

"That so? Marse Bradford know?" asked Henry.

Before Rosa had a chance to reply, Belle, a spirited young girl, sailed into the kitchen from the house. "Not yet he don't. He fine out directly he come down though. I hear him an' Miss El'ner stirrin' roun' upstairs whilst I was settin' de table. He be pleased."

"Who be pleased 'bout what?" asked Henry, hands stretched out toward the warm stove.

"Marse be pleased 'bout de new baby. What else?" Rosa said. "I hear Marse say a while back when Jake was born, any chile a Mable's worth its weight in solid gold. Dat what he say. I hear him, me standin' by de kitchen door, him outside talking wid Tom. Solid gold."

Henry laughed. "Gimme plenty a gravy on my meat an' biscuits so I be fat an' worth a diamon'-studded stick pin."

"Take more than gravy," Belle said as she gave Henry a good-natured push.

"You two quit goshin' an' get to work," said Rosa. "Look at dat cream pitcher. Christmas or no Christmas, Miss El'ner see tarnish roun' de handle she send it flying back here to get de situation remedied or my name ain't Rosa."

"It Rosa," put in Belle. "Han' de pitcher here. I give it a lick an' a promise wid some ashes from de grate an' a dab a vinegar. What you say de baby name?"

"Eliza."

"Eliza," repeated Belle. "Dat pretty soundin'. Real pretty soundin'."

Right then the house bell gangled, and Rosa quickly moved into action. "Dey downstairs, ready fer breakfast. Hand me de platter dere, Belle, so's I can dish up. We mussin' keep dem waitin' on Christmas mornin'."

Belle held on to the blue platter with both hands. "Should I tell dem 'bout de baby whilst I servin'?"

"I reckon so," answered Rosa, forking savory brown rabbit from frying pan to platter. "I'd like to be on han' myself to see Marse's face light up when he hear de news, but wid a goose an' a turkey to stuff an' cook, I bes' stay right here. Go long wid de tray an' mine you don't trip over de sill."

"Yes, ma'am."

Rosa poked Henry saying, "Open de door fer Belle, den carry dis platter in de house fer her. An', Henry, whilst you in de dinin' room, stir de fire an' lay on a fresh log."

"Yes, ma'am."

"An' one thin' more. When you done in de house, see can you fine Steven an' Charles an' tell dem to hitch de horses in plenty a time fer church. I speck dey down de barn 'bout now."

"Yes, ma'am."

Rosa watched the young people go out the door laughing and having a good time together. Alone in the kitchen, she folded her hands, bowed her head, and said aloud, "Merry Christmas, Jesus Lord. Merry Christmas, Eliza Ann Benson."

4

Good Times

The Benson stair steps went like this: Viney, Jonas, Marnie, Lillie and Jake. All were straight-backed, tall, and lean like their mother, Mable. Eliza looked like her father, Tom. She was small-boned, and her dark brown eyes were bright. Her ways were her own. She was determined and stubborn and independent. At the three-week mark she decided she wanted to turn over, and over she went without help from anybody.

Eliza was a rag doll to her big sister Viney. Whirlwind Viney would swoop down on the baby, pick her up, hug her fiercely, then put her back down, and be gone. Early, Eliza learned to adjust to sudden yes and no, sudden here and gone, sudden much and little or nothing.

Born against the backdrop of pre-Civil-War South, Eliza knew who she was, what she was, and why at an early age. Before she could stand alone she knew that the Eastern Shore of Maryland was the best place on earth, not the South, not Maryland—the Eastern Shore. She knew that the choice home on the Eastern Shore was Clay's Hope. She knew that Marse Bradford and his family were her family, though not the way that Tom, Mable, her brothers and sisters, and Rosa (never leave out Rosa) were family. Marse Bradford was home, red brick, and spiritual the way the Episcopal Church was—only different. Nobody told Eliza the things she knew; they were marrow in her bones. She learned them as she nursed at Mable's warm and generous breast. The sun and the rain and the wild geese told her.

When Eliza was ten months old, she stood alone. Before long she was following Viney out to the bean patch where the other children were weeding and talking. Not Jake. He was too little to know a weed from a bean plant. Keep him out of the patch. Keep Eliza out too, or at least on the edge of the patch.

It was Viney who taught Eliza to talk. Oh, she said "Mama" and "Papa" on her own, copying the other children; but words of the wide world she learned from Viney.

"Barn," Viney said sitting back on her tough bare heels in the sandy earth between bean rows. "B-b-barn. Say it, Liza."

"No," Eliza said. She knew that word on her own.

"Say 'barn,' or I'll beat ya. 'B-b-barn.'"

"B-b-barn," Eliza said toppling over, laughing, sure as anything that Viney would never, never beat her—Viney nor anybody else.

Viney laughed loud, head thrown back so the laugh could rise up and scare the blackbirds stealing corn. "Dat's right. You talkin' fin'. Now say 'tree,'" she said, pointing to the oak by the fence. "Tree."

"Tree, tree, tree," Eliza sang out. She got to her feet, which wasn't far to go, short as her legs were.

"Jes fin'," Viney told her. "Watch out fer de bean plants. You step on dem wid your big feet, Marse Bradford take a stick to ya."

Eliza looked down at her small, brown feet, and rocked back and forth and giggled the way Lillie did when Marnie tickled her in the ribs. She knew Marse Bradford wouldn't beat her even if she trampled down the whole patch. Well, he might, the whole patch ruined. He should. A baby knew that much—a smart baby.

On the way back to the house for lunch when the sun was directly overhead, Viney turned to Eliza trudging behind her. "Say 'Sista Viney.'"

"Sista Viney," Eliza said, plain as day. Viney whirled around, picked up the little girl, and ran fast as a rabbit with the hounds after it. She leaped high, hugging Eliza to her and shouted, "Wait fer us, Papa. Wait an' hear Liza say my name!"

Tom stopped near the pump, rested his hoe, and wiped sweat from his forehead with the clean white handerkerchief Mable made for him. Viney, out of breath, set the baby down at his feet. "What my name? Tell Papa my name."

Eliza was overcome with shyness and ducked behind Viney's skinny legs. "Leave her be, Viney," said Tom. "Don't make her do. She too little."

Viney scratched a mosquito bite vigorously. "Make Eliza do? Nobody make her do nothin'; she got a mind a her own like you, Papa."

Tom nodded, pleased. He was proud to have one child take after him. He was proud of all of his children, but Eliza was special. When they got near the house, they could hear Mable calling.

31

A Promise is to Keep

"Tom, you an' Viney hurry 'long now. I got work to do soon's your lunch over. Call de other chillen. I got a kettle a bean soup an' ham bits waitin'. An' cold biscuits to go wid it."

"We comin' Mable."

At Clay's Hope there was always plenty of good food to eat: all the crab you could eat, terrapin to give away, corn, beans, collards, and tomatoes, fresh in season and home-canned out of season. There were always good appetites there too, the product of good health and plenty of work to do for every lad—old, young, slave, or free. With Marse Bradford watching to see that his farm ran smoothly year round, everybody did his best.

Mable washed clothes in tubs set up on saw horses so she didn't have to break her back scrubbing. Fair days in summer she washed out back close to the kitchen door. Rainy and cold days she worked in the shed. Winter and summer, good days and bad, Henry kept a fire going under the big iron boiling kettle over by the sycamore tree.

Eliza liked to watch her mother hang sheets on the line, never a corner touching the ground. From the shade of the lilac bush she'd watch the sheets flapping on the line, white as goose wings. She learned by watching. Best of all she liked to ride home on top of the clothes basket at the end of the day. Mable would spread a clean towel on top of the sweet smelling mound of clothes, then set Eliza on top. Jake ran alongside wanting to ride too, which made the ride even more enjoyable. He was too big to ride; Eliza wasn't.

Sometimes at sunset Mable carried Eliza down to the cove to watch the canvasback ducks, the red heads, the mallards and the geese land for the night. Seeing them, Eliza would squeal with delight. One evening Mable pointed to a sailboat out on the water and said, "That Cousin Willie takin' Miss Em and Miss Mary to a party in town. He escortin' both, but his eye come to res' on Miss Em."

"Em," Eliza said, and Mable corrected her. "Miss Em, honey. T'aint respectful widout de 'Miss.'"

"Miss Em," Eliza said, anxious to please.

"That right."

Every day there was something new to learn and a lot of playing to do with Jake, the pups, and the kittens. Bess, the Chesapeake Bay dog, had six puppies. Suzy, the black cat, had five kittens. Mable had Dan, a new baby. Eliza moved upstairs with the older children. At first she didn't like it up there sleeping between the two middle sisters; soon she liked it fine. Viney was there too, with a pallet on the floor.

Growing up was fun. Once she rode on the wide back of Abraham, a plow horse. Marse Bradford himself put her there, so she wasn't scared much. He wouldn't let any of the children ride Judith or Lafayette or the colt Perry. They were too spirited to be safe. Once Marse piled all of the children, except Dan who was too young for anything, into the carriage. Off they went down the driveway, down the road halfway to town and back, the wheels turning so fast nobody could see the spokes. Eliza would never forget that ride.

The icing on Eliza's cake, though, was Dolly, her rag doll. Mable made Dolly especially for her out of a strip of Miss El'ner's worn-out sheet. She rolled it tight and hard before she sewed it so Dolly would last. She stitched on a friendly face and dressed the doll in purple calico over a full white petticoat.

A Promise is to Keep

Eliza found Dolly entirely satisfactory. In fact, she found everything entirely satisfactory. "It can't last," Rosa said to Mable during a Monday lunch in the big kitchen. Eliza, almost two years old, was sitting on a box on the wooden chair next to her mother, eating a corn cake and listening to the conversation.

"What can't last, Rosa?" Mable asked.

"Good times. Dey been wid Marse Bradford, Miss El'ner an' dem fer a long time. It flyin' in de face a Providence to speck dem to keep on. Things bound to dip. De world go by ups an' downs same as people do. Don't nothin' stay put 'cept God Amighty."

"That so, Rosa," Mable said, pouring herself another cup of tea. After a long pause, Rosa added, "I got a feelin' in my bones we all headin' into a squall. Marse Bradford got a worried look on his face lately. You mark my words, a squall comin'."

Eliza looked up at Rosa and frowned. She knew what a squall was. She'd seen more than one come up fast over the creek. First sign of a cloud she'd head for the house. Viney would too, and the other children. Tom would come in from the field, and Cousin Willie out on the water would head for shore.

With her free hand, the one not holding Dolly, Eliza reached for another corn slapper and stuffed the whole thing in her mouth. Thin as a leaf and edged with lace, it tasted so good.

5

The Deep Dip

Marse Bradford walked slowly on his morning rounds, head bent, arms hanging at his sides heavy as two slabs of bacon. The slave children kept their distance. Usually they ran after him shouting, "Marse, Marse, swing me cross de stream!" Not that day. Even Eliza, young as she was, knew better than to bother him when he had something weighing down his mind.

Marse had plenty on his mind. His wife Eleanor was sick in bed. He was concerned over politics, both national and local, and he did not take lightly his own responsibilities. He was a man of property. Besides Clay's Hope, the dwelling house, he owned "Canton," also called "Crooked Intention," another beautiful farm inherited from his father, and a place called "Cumberland," left to Miss El'ner by her father. Several small houses in the town of St. Michaels were his and a few slaves.

Marse Bradford took good care of his slaves and they took good care of him. That was as it should be, or was it, he wondered. Oh, the caring was fine, but what about one man owning another? He and a group of his friends met from time to time in town to discuss the pros and cons of slavery. They were not alone. Petitions were being sent to Congress from all over the country requesting abolition. A new political party was forming, so the newspapers said, The Liberty Party, composed of moderates interested in abolition not the dissolution of the Union. Once the party was official, Marse Bradford planned to join.

He was not sure what President Van Buren thought about the subject. With inflation, sky-high rent, food prices way up, fuel scarce, a government deficit, and more than one bank unstable, it was all the president could do to keep his head above water. Abolition would have to wait.

Miss El'ner must get well soon. Marse Bradford could not get along without her. Stopping at the pasture fence to give Judith her daily lump of sugar, Marse's spirit rose. Perhaps he was being unduly concerned about his wife. Daughters Mary and Emily were taking such good care of her, surely she would be up and about before long.

Henry in the hay loft saw Marse walking briskly back to the house, head up, arms swinging. He called the good news down to Charles, and in no time everybody was feeling fine again because Marse was. Feeling fine did not last long. Bad news traveled down the back-stairs to the kitchen, out the kitchen door, and on to the quarters—Miss El'ner was worse.

For days the children played quietly. They knew what was what without being told. They had seen the doctor tie his horse at the hitching post every day around noon. "He come then," Viney said, "cause he an' everybody else fer mile around know Rosa's biscuits is de lightes' in de county."

The Deep Dip

Thursday, the second week of Miss El'ner's sickness, Viney heard the doctor tell Marse she was gravely ill. Viney declared she was listening at the sitting room door, saw the doctor and Marse sipping brandy after dinner, and heard what the doctor said with her own ears.

Mary and Emily, worn-out from nursing their mother, now refused to leave her for a moment. They took turns sleeping so one would be on duty night and day. When a neighbor, twenty-year-old Catherine Townsend, came over to help saying she would stay as long as she was needed, the girls welcomed her gratefully. They were both so tired. As Belle carried Miss Catherine's bag up to the guest room, gloom lifted slightly. The house was too quiet. There wasn't a sound except whispering in the hall outside the sickroom door, the tiptoeing up and down the stairs, and the tictoc, tictoc of the grandfather's clock on the landing.

Marse Bradford paced the study floor. He was letting the farm run itself the best way it could without him. His sons Samuel and Jonathan were away at college. His daughters were nearly grown women now with lives of their own. He felt lonely. The thought that he might lose Miss El'ner brought him to his knees.

Early in the evening Henry's dog howled and howled out beyond the tobacco field. Tom Benson, sitting on a stool by his fire, was whittling a boat for little Jake, who stood close watching. Tom heard the howling. He rested his knife and said to his wife Mable, "Spot, he talkin' to de moon."

Mable looked up from her sewing and said, "He talkin' to de angel a' death, Tom. He tell him go somewheres else." She laid her sewing aside, leaned over the cradle beside her, and tucked the pink blanket in around baby Dan. The baby stirred. She bent her head, closed her eyes, and prayed silently for all of her children, Viney on down to Eliza and Dan, and one on its way.

That night, March 4, 1838, Eleanor Spencer Harrison died.

The next morning Jonas, Marnie, Lilly, Jake, and Eliza holding on to Viney by the hand stood in a solemn row watching Henry dig the grave down on the bank of the creek not far from the dock. Two small graves were already there, graves of Miss El'ner's dead babies. One, her first-born, lived only twenty days, so the stone marker said.

The children stood there big-eyed, watching with macabre interest the shovelfuls of fresh earth fly up and land in a mound. Rosa's grandsons, Charles and Steven, were big enough to help with the digging. They leaned on their shovels and talked about the scary mystery of death.

Eliza was too young to be scared. She let go of her big sister's hand, stepped close to the grave, leaned way over, and looked down. If Viney hadn't grabbed her, she'd have toppled in.

Henry lined the grave with bricks, selecting one at a time from the stack by the dock. There were plenty, brought over from England as ballast in trading ships to trade for American tobacco. Bricking was too slow. The children soon lost interest and ran off to the quarters, shouting, chasing one another, full of life. Death was for other people, sick people, old people—not for them.

Everybody, young and old, attended the funeral, though the children couldn't see much, only the backs of grownups standing in front of them. They could hear the sonorous voice of Cousin Joseph Spencer, Rector of Christ Episcopal Church, reading the service. "In the midst of life we are in death." Viney, awed by the mighty words, let out a primitive wail, for which she got a sharp rebuke from her mother. "Hush up. You want people to think you don't know nothin' 'bout nothin' ?"

The wail and the rebuke were too much for Eliza. She howled loud and lustily and kept on howling until Viney picked her up and toted her fast out of earshot. The silent weeping of the family must not be disturbed by Eliza's goings on.

Poor Marse Bradford. Although his sorrow was deep, living had to go on. In time he packed his mourning away like an old coat and shouldered his responsibilities once again. Things went along as usual at Clay's Hope, Mary and Emily taking their mother's place. Or so they thought. Not so. On the first day of October the following year, 1839, Alexander Bradford Harrison and Catherine Townsend were married.

According to one of my mother's cousins, Mr. Harrison's children were not pleased. They were fond of their father's new wife as a friend and neighbor, were grateful to her for all she had done for their mother, but they did not need or want a stepmother. They were old enough to look after themselves and their father. And they said so to one another. Not to their father, though. They would not have dared to question his judgment.

The servants had plenty to say behind closed doors. "Better aired out dan kep' inside," Rosa declared, then added. "Keep your voice down, Viney. You an' Belle been cacklin' like a couple a hens since sunup. How come you set yourselves up to criticize Marse? You don't know what he need. He fifty years old an' he got burdens to carry. He need somebody to hep him."

Mable came in the back door with a basketful of clean clothes and spoke her piece. "Miss Cathern suit him fin' an' she suit me fin' an' in time she suit you all fin'. Ain't nobody got a right to look down dey nose at her. She born gentle an' she reared gentle an' she smart. I know. Didn't I rock her when she a baby befo' Marse Bradford bought me from her father fer Tom? Marse know what he doin'."

"Mable right," Rosa said, nodding her head. "Marse know what he doin' an' anybody got a word to say against him or her belong somewheres else."

Everybody agreed to that in the kitchen and out in the fields from Rosa herself on down to Eliza and even to Dan, still too new to hold up his own head.

Anne Catherine Bradford Harrison—Eliza's "Miss Braddie"—was conceived in the four poster and born on February 12, 1841. How she came to be Eliza's was Marse Bradford's idea. Six adults in the house not counting the servants and one baby would not do. A baby needed laughter and singing around the cradle.

Marse Bradford, alone in his study, turned the thought over in his mind and came up with a splendid idea. He'd give four-year-old Eliza Benson to his daughter Braddie to live with her side by side as friend and slave. He would never sell a slave child away from her home and family, but this was different. Clay's Hope was Eliza's home. Belonging to Braddie she'd still be home, still see her parents every day, and her brothers and sisters too.

The idea pleased him. He would tend to it at once.

6

Miss Braddie

That night while taking off his boots and getting ready for bed, Marse Bradford told his wife about his decision to give Eliza Ann to the baby. She was delighted and wanted the little girl brought to the house right away. Pulling his night shirt over his handsome head, Marse Bradford declared he'd fetch the child himself first thing in the morning.

Belle, who was getting an extra blanket out of the chest in the hall, couldn't help hearing her master and mistress talking. So by the time Marse set foot on Tom's doorstep the next day, the entire Benson family already knew what he'd come to say.

Mable and Tom were pleased and proud as peacocks to think they'd have a daughter living in the dwelling house. Eliza Ann was not pleased at first. She wanted to stay where she was—with her brothers and sisters. She soon changed her mind, though; rather Viney changed it for her. "How come Marse choose Eliza Ann 'stead of me?" Viney asked in a peeved tone. "She only four an' can't even play hopscotch widout steppin' on de lines."

And Lilly threw coals on the fire by saying, "Why not me?" And Marnie said, "Or me?" adding envy to envy.

41

Eliza Ann eyed her sisters and saw herself in a new light. She was somebody special, a gift to the baby, a gift to Marse Bradford's own child, and they were not. She was "it," and they wanted to be. Eliza Ann did some figuring in her head. She had to go because Marse said so, and what he said everybody did because they were his. How she minded was up to her. Very well, then, she'd go willingly, proudly, and alone, not holding anybody by the hand.

The next afternoon Eliza Ann left her parents' warm crowded home in the quarters, her mother's red wool shawl around her shoulders, Dolly in her arms. She walked up the path to the dwelling house and stood outside the back door. She wanted to go in but couldn't for shyness. She waited until the door opened and Rose said, "Come on in, honey. Your sister Viney in the pantry wiping off the shelves." She raised her voice, "Viney, here Liza Ann. Come take her up to the baby's room and mind you don't make a racket on the stairs."

"Yes, ma'am."

"Wait," Rosa said as the girls started for the door. "Han' me Mable's shawl. I'll take it back to her later on. Liza Ann won't be needin' it no more. She be wearin' new clothes from now on. Miss Mary an' Miss Em'ly got thimbles on a'ready."

Hugging Dolly in both arms, Eliza Ann followed Viney out of the kitchen, into the house, and up the back stairs, her heart pounding harder than it ever had before. She followed Viney along the upstairs hall to the front bedroom. Viney tapped lightly on the door, Eliza Ann standing there sure-footed, expecting her heart would burst.

"Come in."

The next thing Eliza Ann knew, she was leaning over

the cradle. There was the baby sound asleep. Her baby. She'd never forget the first sight of Miss Braddie, not much bigger than Dolly, face pink as a rose bud, a wisp of straight black hair sticking out from under the smallest lace cap in the world. Eliza Ann leaned closer. The baby had little bitty dark eye lashes. She could see them dark against her soft, soft cheeks and she had the tenderest little hands.

Marse Bradford gave Eliza Ann to Miss Braddie— that was one thing. Eliza Ann gave herself, which was entirely different. It was grand as the sky, clear as the spring. Forever she would be Miss Braddie's; forever Miss Braddie would be hers.

Viney, watching her little sister bending over the cradle, sensed a covenant in the air, a promise with the Good Lord in it. Not part of it, she tiptoed out of the room and down the back stairs.

From that moment on Eliza Ann stayed close to her baby night and day. She slept beside her in the trundle bed Miss Catherine pulled out from under the big bed. She put her clothes in the bottom bureau drawer, Miss Braddie's things in the other drawers. She held a warm towel ready to hand to Miss Catherine after the baby's bath. She emptied the bath water into the slop jar that Belle would carry down to the necessary house.

Sometimes while Miss Braddie was taking her nap Eliza Ann visited her parents in the quarters, played catchers and hi-spy with her brothers and sisters, and compared Mable's new baby, Bea, with her baby. Once Miss Catherine let Eliza Ann hold her baby on her lap, rock her in the little rocking chair Marse Bradford made years ago for his first-born. He made the cherry high chair in the dining room too, empty for years now. It wouldn't be empty long, though. Miss Braddie would be sitting in it soon, fast as she was growing.

A Promise is to Keep

Marse Bradford was handy with tools. In his spare time he liked to work in the tool shed, Tom there with him holding up one end of a board while he sawed off the other end. He and Tom talked as they worked. They were good friends. Marse told Tom about a new invention, a reaper, that could do as much work in one day as ten men. They talked about shipbuilding, the backbone of the country, and farming, the business of buying and selling at home and abroad, tobacco mostly around home, in the wider market, cotton. Once the conversation landed on cotton, it quickly drifted to the worrisome web of politics.

Tom found it hard to believe that cotton was dividing the country and also the South. Fond of big words, he told Marse he was sure they'd both live to see time "rectify the inequities." Tom lived that long, but Marse didn't.

In fiction death can be moved here and there to suit the plot of the story or left out altogether. In a true story like Eliza Ann's, it barges in ruthlessly to shatter the plot, to scatter the people, to lay a heavy hand on children. When Miss Braddie was only two months old, Marse Bradford died. It was sad to see another white marble slab on the bank of the creek beside Miss El'ner's:

> Alexander Bradford Harrison
> Died: April 12, 1841
> Age: Fifty-one years, six months,
>   and twenty-nine days,

carved deep.

Miss Braddie was too young to mourn for him. All she knew or needed was Eliza Ann and her mother.

Eliza Ann was not too young to mourn in her own way. To her, Marse Bradford under the ground instead of walking on it was the candle blown out, dark night all around. To her, Marse gone was singing and laughter gone too.

At the reading of the will in the sitting room, Miss Mary, Miss Em, Master Samuel and Master Jonathan sat on straight chairs in front of the lawyer. Miss Catherine sat in the black easy chair behind Miss Mary, Eliza Ann standing beside her, hand on the arm of the chair.

Behind the family stood all the servants except Belle, who was minding the baby, and Viney, who was minding her baby sister Bea, Dan, and Jake.

After the resounding "Considering the uncertainty of life and the never-erring certainty of death," the lawyer read, 'I, Alexander Bradford Harrison . . . give and bequeath to my son Samuel the farm Crooked Intention, adjoining the town of St. Michaels . . ." on and on. Then, "I give and bequeath to my son Jonathan my dwelling house and the farm attached, Clay's Hope. Also to Jonathan his grandfather Spencer's eight-day clock and his grandfather Harrison's never-to-be-parted-with cane and two black boys, Stephen and Charles, to serve until they are thirty-one years old and then to be set free."

Eliza Ann liked that part about home and the boys and the clock and the cane. It was as though Marse were still there talking. He gave a farm to each of his daughters, Mary and Emily, which also pleased Eliza Ann. But what she liked best was when the lawyer read, "I give to my old and faithful servant, Rosa, for her great attention to me and my family, the house and lot whereon she lives together with a sufficiency of firewood to be cut and hauled to her door. And all of my Negroes not heretofore provided for shall be divided between my four children to serve until they are thirty-one years old and then to be set free."

Miss Catherine, Miss Braddie and Eliza Ann were mentioned in a codicil of the will because the second marriage took place after the writing of the will and Miss Catherine did not want it to be changed. In the codicil, she was to continue to live at Clay's Hope as long as she wanted with money to live on during her life. To his daughter Anne Catherine Bradford Harrison—Miss Braddie—Marse left three thousand dollars and Eliza Ann. So Eliza Ann was Miss Braddie's three ways now: by the spoken word, by the written word, and by solemn covenant.

"What 'bout Mama an' Papa?" Eliza Ann asked Rosa when they were back in the kitchen. "De man didn't read a word 'bout dem."

"No need to, honey." Rosa told her. "Tom, he free a'ready an' Mable be free come September. Marse tell Tom whilst he sick in bed soon as de chillen old enough to leave behin', a house waitin' fer him an' Mable in St. Michaels. He tell Tom all he an' Mable got to do to get a job as free people was to sit by de door. Fin' as dey were an' well turned-out, somebody would rap on it befo' sundown."

Belle came into the kitchen just then saying, "Eliza Ann, you standin' dere doin' nothin', an' Miss Braddie awake an' lookin' fer ya."

Eliza Ann ran to the door, into the house, up the back stairs as fast as she could run, calling out, "I'm a comin', Miss Braddie." Nobody had to rap on her door, now or ever.

7

The Accident

Clay's Hope mourned for Marse Bradford. Miss Catherine, dressed in black without even a touch of white around her slender, white neck, wrote letters, poured tea for callers in the parlor, rocked her baby, and sewed. The girls Miss Mary and Miss Em, also in black, stayed indoors most of the time going to town only to attend church on Sunday. Occasionally close friends came to visit.

Viney and Belle swapped yarns in the pantry as usual. They kept their voices low, partly out of respect for the family, but mostly because Rosa would take a carpet beater to them if they didn't. Rosa herself was full of scary tales about ghosts. She declared she wouldn't be surprised to see Marse Bradford's ghost walking around the place any day. "Much as he cared 'bout Clay's Hope, he boun' to keep a eye on it. An' dem runnin' it now better toe de lin'."

The horses still looked over the fence, ears pointed, hoping to see Marse coming with a sugar lump on his outstretched hand or a carrot held out. The dogs still listened for his step. The young children played on the creek side of the quarters so they wouldn't disturb the family. The big children went about the business of learning a trade.

One afternoon Viney carried Miss Braddie, dressed to show off in a lace-trimmed long dress and matching cap, down to the quarters. Eliza, wearing the new red plaid dress Miss Em made for her, skipped ahead shouting, "Here she come. Here come Miss Braddie!"

Mable must have heard the commotion, for she was there waiting on the doorstep, white apron on. "Um, mmm," she said, taking the baby from Viney. "She pretty as a mockingbird. Eye's blacker than Eliza's. Look, she smilin' at me." She held the baby out arm's length to get a better look and said, "She put me in mind a Marse Bradford."

"She do fer fair," Viney said, and Eliza, overcome with pride, nodded her round head yes, yes, yes. The other children who had gathered around by this time each had something to say on the subject. Marnie said the baby looked like any other baby, only she was white. Jonas said she looked like a calf he had once. Lilly hit him saying, "She does not, she's beautiful!" Slow Jake, chewing on a sassafras root, didn't say anything.

"Viney! Viney!" Rosa called from the house. "Come back here an' finish dustin' de parlor. Anybody know how to write his name could write it on de piano."

"We comin'."

Eliza skipped ahead of her big sister and the baby. The other children who were always ready to play follow the leader skipped behind, imitating Eliza. Even in the midst of mourning, playing was hard to keep down.

The Accident

When Miss Braddie was six months old, she sat up alone. In no time she was sitting in the high chair, banging on the dining room table with her spoon. When she was a year old she walked, holding Eliza's hand. She said her first word, "Liza," which was enough to make Eliza hide her face with her hands she was so proud.

When Miss Braddie was three years old, Mable made a rag doll for her just like Eliza's Dolly. The new doll was called Celia. While Miss Catherine, Miss Mary and Miss Em were busy sewing things of beauty for two hope chests, Eliza, Miss Braddie, Dolly and Celia played house on the landing of the front stair. Eliza was an expert at pretending, and it didn't take Miss Braddie long to catch on.

Warm days the girls played in the barn or went wading in the stream. Every day, cold or warm, rainy or clear, they played in the corner of the kitchen listening to Rosa tell stories and sing songs. Eliza liked to hear about the time General Lafayette visited Maryland. "A fin' gentleman he were," Rosa said. "No wonder Marse Bradford name his horse Lafayette."

"Did you see him?" Eliza asked every time Rosa told the story. And every time Rosa answered, "Not wid my eyes. But I hear 'bout him 'til I see him widout dem. Marse Bradford, he saw him wid his eyes."

All of the children played hard out in the quarters. Miss Braddie, young as she was, kept up as well as she could. Home sheep run, hi-spy, king of the mountain— Miss Braddie came in last but got there nonetheless, and Eliza cheered her on.

The year Eliza was nine going on ten, two weddings took place at Clay's Hope. Miss Mary married The

A Promise is to Keep

Reverend J. Ruth and moved to Philadelphia. Miss Em married Willie Harrison, her full-of-fun, devoted-since-the-day-one, second cousin Willie. They settled down at "Mount Pleasant," a beautiful farm two miles from St. Michaels.

For weeks after the weddings, the children played weddings. Dolly and Celia, dressed in long trains and veils made from scraps of lace and voile found under the sewing table, were brides. Good days the weddings were held in the small boxwood garden out back of the dwelling house with Marnie, Lillie, Jake, several cats, a couple of hunting dogs, and now and then a goose attending.

Eliza, wearing a folded crib sheet around her shoulders, stood on a wooden box and officiated as minister. Imitating Cousin Joe Spencer's deep voice, she said, "Dearly beloved, we are gathered here in de sight a God . . . " She raised her voice to a shout: "Viney, what come after 'de sight a God?'"

Viney poked her head out the kitchen door and answered, "Dum, dum-de-dum," pretending to be the organ. The children giggled and giggled. Those days the least little thing, even just being together, would set them giggling.

Then the accident happened and there was no more giggling at Clay's Hope. Henry blamed the ground hog. Charles said it was the black snake's fault, and Stephen agreed saying, "That de one done it. Black snake de one." Rosa said if Lafayette hadn't stepped in the ground hog hole he wouldn't have sprained his ankle. If he hadn't sprained his ankle, he would have been hitched to the carriage with Judith where he belonged. "It warn't Perry's fault. He young, skittish, an' a ridin' horse. He not used to harness," Tom said.

The Accident

Ground hog, snake, Lafayette or Perry—the accident happened.

Miss Catherine, still in mourning black, though handsome nonetheless, was driving. Miss Braddie sat beside her mother, her beautiful, calm oval face out of sight in a pink poke bonnet. Eliza was in her best dress, a dusty blue calico with tiny white daisies, and she sat on the other side of Miss Braddie. She did not have on a bonnet, but she wore blue ribbons on her plaits, two on each side tied together to make one. Both girls wore full petticoats, white stockings and black leather slippers that came from England on a trading ship. They were on their way over to the Townsend farm to have tea with Grandma Amelia Applegarth Townsend, but they never got there.

Just before the carriage reached the Clay's Hope gate, a black snake long as a buggy whip crossed the road right in front of the horses. Perry snorted and reared. Judith, startled by the snake and confused by Perry, reared also. The carriage tipped, spilling Miss Catherine and the children, then righted, and the horses bolted.

Eliza and Miss Braddie set up such a howl that Henry heard it in the hayloft of the barn. He came running as fast as he could, pitchfork in hand. Panting, he caught up with Rosa, Belle, and Viney as they flew down the driveway, apron strings flapping.

The girls were not seriously hurt. They were plenty scared, though, and their elbows were skinned. "Dere now, dere now," Rosa said, comforting them while Viney and Belle helped them to their feet, brushing off their skirts.

"Take de chillen back to de house, Viney, you an'

Belle," Henry ordered. "Miss Rosa, stay an' hep me wid Miss Cathern."

Catherine Townsend Harrison, lying face down on the side of the road, did not move or cry out. Her breast bone was crushed. Before long, in spite of constant and loving care by Rosa, Mable, Belle and Viney, Miss Catherine died in the four poster.

"Poor Miss Cathern, only twenty-six year old," Rosa said, weeping and weeping.

"Poor Miss Braddie," Mable said. "Only six year old an' mother an' father both gone."

"She not alone, though," Rosa said. "She got Eliza."

"She do, indeedy," Mable said. "Marse know what he was doin' by givin' my child Eliza to his child. He knew."

8

Mount Pleasant

Eliza wouldn't talk about what happened next, but two sentences from an old letter pared down that year to the bone: "After the death of her mother, Braddie Harrison and a servant girl, Eliza, went to live with Uncle William Townsend's daughter. The girls were not happy there."

Would they have been happy anywhere, missing Clay's Hope and the people who lived there—Mable, Tom, Rosa, Viney and the rest? One guess. Anyway, when Miss Em heard that the girls were unhappy, she invited them to live at Mount Pleasant Farm with her, her husband Cousin Willie, and their two-year-old daughter, Nellie.

The invitation was accepted at once. Miss Braddie had been over to Mount Pleasant several times. Once to see Nellie when she was brand new, twice to ride the pony Pudgy, and once to a grown-up tea to meet Miss Caroline Denny, the young woman her brother Jonathan was courting. Eliza had never been there, but she felt as though she had from the glowing picture of it painted by Miss Braddie. "The brick house is smaller than the dwelling house at Clay's Hope, Liza. It is beautiful, though, with big trees on a wide lawn down to the water."

Nobody had to tell Eliza anything about the people at Mount Pleasant. She knew Miss Em and Cousin Willie like the back of her hand. As for Miss Nellie, she was a little girl, wasn't she? Eliza needed no introduction to anybody young or any animal young. Black or white or yellow or red, she knew babies.

It was raining the day Cousin Willie came to fetch the girls, and Miss Braddie had a cold. Nevertheless, spirits were high as he stowed bundles, boxes, and satchels in the back of the buggy. "Up you go," he swung Miss Braddie, clutching Celia, to the middle of the driver's seat. Once Eliza—Dolly in one hand, pink china pig in the other—landed beside Miss Braddie, Cousin Willie hopped in and off they went. The horse, head held high, trotted clop, clop along the muddy road, his wet back shiny as a seal's, his harness buckles bright as Christmas tree ornaments.

Just beyond St. Michaels, Miss Braddie sneezed "Achoo!" on the horse's tail. Eliza giggled for the first time in ages and said, "Mind how you give him a cold, Miss Braddie." Miss Braddie giggled at that, and Cousin Willie laughed so loud he scared the horse into a fast run.

"Hoo there, Fleet, hoo!"

Cousin Willie was easygoing and fun. Eliza looked forward to living at his house, and living there was going to be fine for Miss Braddie, just fine. It was a shame Miss Braddie's nose was red, and her eyes watery. Eliza admired that straight, sensitive nose and those black eyes when they weren't ailing. Oh well, she'd be pretty again soon, and after all, Miss Em was her sister, not a stranger to impress.

A mile and a half on down the road the horse turned in the wide gate of Mount Pleasant, trotted down the long driveway and around the circle.

"Whoa!" The buggy stopped in front of the house. Cousin Willie stepped down and swung Miss Braddie over to the step. Then he swung Eliza over, calling cheerfully, "Em, Nellie, we're home."

Right away Miss Em opened the front door; little Nellie held onto her skirt, peeking around to see who was there and hopefully not be seen. Eliza smiled at Nellie and held out her hand to the little girl who said, "No!" ducking out of sight behind the skirt.

Eliza smiled at Miss Em. She'd forgotten how handsome Miss Em was, handsome and almost as tall as Cousin Willie. She was no match for Miss Braddie's white skin and black hair kind of beauty; still, she was a good-looking woman, no doubt about that.

Miss Em kissed her sister, saying, "Don't cry, dear. You'll like living here with us as soon as you get used to it. Don't cry."

Before Miss Braddie had a chance to say she wasn't crying, just had watery eyes, Eliza explained: "She got a cold in her nose, Miss Em. Dat's why she isn't pretty. She want to come here to live. We both do. Seein' you an' Cousin Willie like comin' back home. It is, isn't it, Miss Braddie?"

"Achoo!" was Miss Braddie's answer, and Miss Em was quick to say, "A cold and out in all this damp weather. Come in the house this minute." She led the way, stepping swiftly. "Light us a fire in the fireplace, Cousin Willie. Summer or not, it will feel good." She raised her voice: "Han-nah, tea please, and cambric tea for the children."

Sixteen-year-old Hannah, Rosa's granddaughter, appeared in the sitting room doorway at once, wiping her hands on her checked apron. "Cake wid de tea, Miss Em?"

"Toast. And Hannah, how many times have I told you an apron is not a towel. You know my sister and Eliza."

"Yes, ma'am, Miss Em, an' I'm glad to see you. How de do, Miss Braddie. How de do, Eliza Ann. About de apron now . . ." A shout out back switched her train of thought. "I hear Boon callin' Cousin Willie," she said. "Mebbe de horse broke loose on de way to de barn."

Cousin Willie lost no time finding out. A moment later they heard him shout, "Em, you and the children come see the rainbow. It's a beauty."

Eliza never forgot that rainbow. It was double, two beautiful bows one above the other, across the western sky beyond the water. A sign from God Himself that from now on, troubles were over for Miss Braddie. As soon as the cold was over, which would be very soon, she was sure.

"It fer you, Miss Braddie," Eliza said and Miss Braddie answered, "Achoo!" Eliza turned to Miss Em. "You bes' put her to bed, rub her chest wid camphor oil, an' cover it wid flannel to keep in de heat."

Miss Em replied coolly, "I am perfectly capable of taking care of my sister, Eliza. Go help Hannah in the kitchen."

"Yes, Miss Em. I know you know what to do, only I been lookin' out fer Miss Braddie night an' day, waitin' on her han' an' foot, so it stan' to reason I know bes' what she need."

"That will do," Miss Em snapped. "It is well seen you have had no training whatever."

Head down from the rebuke, Eliza went in the house. As the door shut she heard Cousin Willie say, "Must you clamp down on her today, Em? After all, she's only a child."

The kitchen smelled like home, a good spice smell. And there was Boon grinning at her. He was tall, thin, and . . . free. "Don't look so hang dog, Eliza Ann. Miss Em, she strict, but she fair. Tell her it so, Hannah."

"It so," replied Hannah. Handing the butter plate to Eliza she added, "Spread de bread not too thin, not too thick an' to de crust. Miss Em, she like it dat way."

Eliza buttered bread, her lower lip stuck out. Her feelings were hurt, and she was angry too. Miss Em was Marse Bradford's own child. She knew better than to call somebody down in front of other people. It wasn't Eliza's fault she'd never been trained. Trained or not, she wasn't stupid. She knew a whole lot about a great many different things. Miss Braddie did, too, because everything Eliza knew she told Miss Braddie, and everything Miss Braddie knew she told Eliza.

They knew who was President of the United States now and before now: Mr. Polk now, and Mr. Tyler before him, and before Mr. Tyler, Mr. William Henry Harrison. Eliza heard that, and what she heard she remembered. She'd never been to school but she knew things. She knew a man named Mr. Howe invented a machine that sewed by a foot pedal, making the needle go up and down. It was hard to believe but true. Another true thing she'd heard about was Morse telegraph. However it worked, she didn't know exactly. Miss Braddie said with it people could talk with other people on the other side of the world.

She and Miss Braddie both thought the most remarkable new discovery was ether. By breathing it, people would go to sleep and sleep so soundly a doctor could cut them wide open and they would not feel it. The world was a wonderful place, and people were smart. Right now the newest thing to do was to pack all of one's belongings in a wagon and head west for California. Eliza wouldn't want to leave the Eastern Shore ever. But if Miss Braddie left she'd leave. Wherever Miss Braddie went, she'd go, like it or not.

The butter job finished, her first job at Mount Pleasant, Eliza opened the kitchen door and stood looking out. The rain had stopped; the rainbow was almost gone. Tomorrow was going to be fair.

The next day was fair, but Miss Braddie's cold was worse. She stayed in bed, Miss Em's orders, and coughed and coughed. The day after that the cold had settled deep in her chest. One horse trotted down the driveway, Boon in the saddle, riding him to town. Before long two horses galloped back—Boon on one, the doctor on the other.

Miss Braddie had pneumonia.

Eliza and little Nellie stood outside the sickroom door like pups waiting to get in. They weren't allowed in, Miss Em's orders. Miss Em would do the nursing, thank you.

Remembering other closed sickroom doors, Eliza was scared.

"Nellie, go along with Eliza," Miss Em said.

Nellie shook her head, frowned, and said, "No."

Eliza stooped and held out her hand to the little girl saying softly, "Come on, honey. Miss Em, she takin' care a Miss Braddie. Come on an' we play."

Nellie shook her head no again and turned away. Then Eliza said, "Dis mornin' I hear Hannah say she fixin' to make biscuits fer supper. I speck she give us enough dough to make a pan a doll bread. We can cut dem wid a thimble, doll size. Want to? Let's us hurry down to de kitchen 'fore it too late an' make us some doll biscuits an' cook 'em an' eat 'em."

The frown melted from Miss Nellie's face. With confidence she took Eliza's hand and walked beside her, taking little girl steps down the stairs, down the hall, and out to the kitchen.

9

Putting Down New Roots

In the daytime Eliza ran errands for Hannah, carrying trays to the sickroom door. Between errands she and her new, devoted friend, Miss Nellie, played with blocks on the side porch or walked down to the water to watch Cousin Willie work on his sail boat, *The Emily H.*

Nights were miserable. Eliza lay wide awake on a narrow cot in Hannah's room fretting to be near Miss Braddie. She knew Miss Em was taking good care of her, but even so, Eliza wanted to be on hand to make sure every last thing that could be done was being done. Besides, Mount Pleasant wasn't home yet. She still felt uprooted. Thinking about Clay's Hope didn't help, either. She didn't even know who was running it now. From bits of news picked up here and there, Master Jonathan had turned the farm over to some stranger and he'd gone off to help Texas fight Mexico. Something about the border between the two was making both sides fighting mad, so she heard. And Master Samuel Alexander hadn't finished medical school. According to what she also heard, getting to be a doctor was a long, hard job.

Putting Down New Roots

Eliza didn't even know whether Tom and Mable were still at Clay's Hope or whether they had moved to town. Once things settled down, maybe Cousin Willie would drive her over to find out what was what. She'd dearly like to see Mable, Tom, Rosa, Viney, and the rest. She really missed them. Still, as Rosa said, weigh what you have against what you don't have. Eliza did that. She had Miss Braddie. Weighed against all else, Miss Braddie was enough.

Suppose Miss Braddie should die like Marse Bradford, Miss El'ner, and Miss Cathern. The thought was unbearable. Eliza got out of bed, opened the door softly so as not to wake Miss Nellie, crossed the hall, and tapped on Miss Em's door.

"What is it?"

"Miss Braddie goin' to be all right, ain't she, Miss Em?"

"Yes."

Eliza went back to bed and went right to sleep. Miss Em's yes was yes.

Ten days later—Sunday it was—Miss Braddie surprised everybody except Miss Em, who was in on the secret. She came down to dinner. Eliza was helping Hannah serve: Hannah handing around the fried chicken, Eliza the gravy. Eliza came into the dining room with the gravy boat on its small silver tray, and there sat Miss Braddie. Pale, thin, her long hair tied back behind her ears, her eyes big and black, she looked beautiful to Eliza, somewhat like a plucked pullet, but beautiful all the same.

"Serve on the left, Eliza," Miss Em said as though it were an ordinary day. "Remove plates from the right, serve on the left."

A Promise is to Keep

"I keep forgettin' which is which," Eliza said, the gravy boat skidding across the tray. "Miss Em, now Miss Braddie well, kin I take care a her from now on?" She looked across the table at Miss Braddie, and the gravy boat toppled, spilling the gravy on the white tablecloth.

Eliza dropped the tray, burst into tears, and bolted. Miss Braddie hurried after her as fast as she could on wobbly legs.

"Come back here at once, both of you!" Miss Em ordered.

The girls returned to the dining room: Eliza blowing her nose, Miss Braddie saying, "She didn't mean to do it, Em. She's a very careful person," which brought on fresh weeping from Eliza.

Ignoring the remark, Miss Em said, "Quit weeping, Eliza. Don't ever waste tears over an accident that hurts no one. And while we are discussing what not to do, a well-trained servant never asks a personal question while serving."

Before Eliza could say yes ma'am, Cousin Willie hopped up and kissed his wife on top of the head saying, "A well-trained husband always does what pleases his wife and mine likes to be kissed. She does, doesn't she, Em?"

He was so funny. Eliza laughed aloud feeling pretty sure a well-trained servant shouldn't. Back in the kitchen she said to Hannah: "Miss Em, she like dat kiss. She pretend she don't but she do. I could tell by de way she duck her head so nobody could see her face." Her mood changed, and she added, "Miss Braddie look like spirit's playmate. She no match fer Hawkins come winter."

Putting Down New Roots

Miss Em must have thought the same thing, for she decided to teach her sister at home that year rather than send her to school at St. Michaels two miles away. She would teach Eliza also. A ten-year-old girl was too old to attend the nearby elementary school for Negro children. Miss Em was not pleased with the school anyway. In the three short years they were there, the pupils learned to read and write simple words and do simple sums. They learned little else. To Miss Em's way of thinking, that was not enough. She was always on a soap box holding forth about the "crying need for better public schools," a phrase her father used many times when he took to a soap box.

Miss Em was a good teacher, and the girls were smart and quick to learn. Braddie soon learned to read stories in the primer, both English and French. She learned to add and subtract and multiply. What she liked best, though, was playing the piano. She'd practice scales by the hour, singing as she played, "do, re, me, fa." Eliza stopped whatever she was doing, dusting or making beds, to listen.

Later in the kitchen she bragged about Miss Braddie's accomplishments. "Miss Em givin' her a piece fer both han's next," she told Hannah, Boon and his wife, and Pink, the cook. Pink, a woman from the Virgin Islands, was free as a storm. She had a quick temper and little patience with children. Even so, she taught Eliza to make sugar cookies and white sauce for green peas.

Eliza was eager to know everything that came down the pike except reading and writing. She refused to learn to read and write, positively would not learn to read and write. Under pressure from the entire family, she gave in enough to learn to write her own name, Eliza Ann Benson, that was all she'd do then or any other time. Her reasoning was her own, sort of a form of pride.

"Miss Braddie do de readin' an' writin' fer both of us," she told Miss Em. "I do other things fer both of us, she read an' write fer both of us."

Miss Em tried and tried to break down the stone wall and so did Miss Braddie and Cousin Willie. They might as well have told the incoming tide to go out. Eliza's mind was made up, and that was that. It was made up about something else, too. She would not go sailing in Cousin Willie's skiff *The Emily H.*

"Storm come up will fin' me on solid ground," she said.

She liked to go crabbing, though, and so did Miss Braddie. Early in the morning, the two of them would start out barefoot, skirts tucked up, Miss Braddie carrying the crab net, Eliza the bucket. They'd stalk along the edge of the inlet, silent and alert as two herons, eyes quick to see the slightest motion in the water. Usually when Cousin Willie blew the fog horn at the back door to signal that breakfast was ready, the bucket would be at least half-full.

Both girls liked to sew; all three after Eliza taught Miss Nellie how to hem a handkerchief for her father. The wide, uneven stitches taken lovingly with a large darning needle were given lots of praise, which delighted the very young seamstress.

The sewing bees took place in the guest room at the end of the upstairs hall, the sewers talking and singing songs that Mable and Rosa taught Eliza.

64

"It was Christmas Eve, 1836, cold and clear in Talbot County on the Eastern Shore of Maryland. The lamp in the dwelling house at Clay's Hope had been blown out."

"Between the water and the dwelling house stood the quarters. A candle was burning in the second house where Tom Benson lived—Tom and Mabel."

"A mile and a half down the road the horse turned in the wide gate of Mount Pleasant, and trotted down the driveway and around the circle.

" 'Whoa!' The buggy stopped in front of the house."

A photograph of Miss Braddie taken for Edward to acknowledge their engagement. Braddie sent it to Edward in 1860 at his urging.

Edward's college photograph from Princeton, 1855, sent to Braddie in return as an engagement photograph.

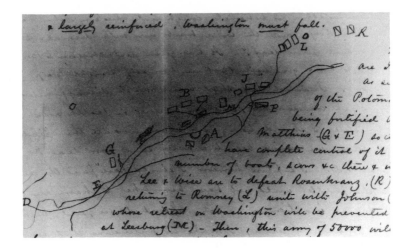

Letters from Edward Spencer to Miss Braddie. The first letter is dated August 13, 1861, Tuesday night (above). It includes Edward's battle plans and diagrams for preventing the invasion of Maryland by Union troops. The second letter also shows how closely Edward followed the war, even in love notes to his beloved Braddie (below).

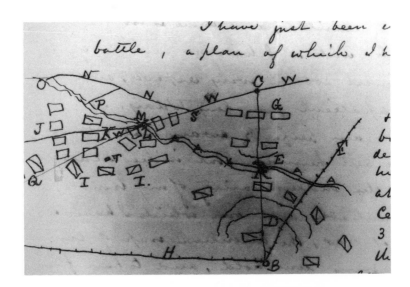

"This time tomorrow, the Lord willing, the Spencer family, all of them—Miss Braddie, Mr. Edward, and Eliza—would be home at The Martin's Nest, near Randallstown."

Mr. Edward Spencer in his later years, 1880 or 1881, not long before his death.

Mr. McCoy

"After a long silence the heavyset gentleman in the back of the courtroom stood up and asked for permission to speak.

"'Granted, Mr. McCoy,' the judge said, nodding his head with approval."

The Haydens lived at Nancy's Fancy with their three girls—Ruth, Catherine, Nan—from 1906 until 1946. Eliza lived here until she died.

Eliza, her face full of wisdom and determination (Courtesy of the Maryland Historical Society)

"Eliza, short, rounded, small-boned, and cinnamon brown"—
posing in the doorway of the little stone house at Nancy's Fancy.

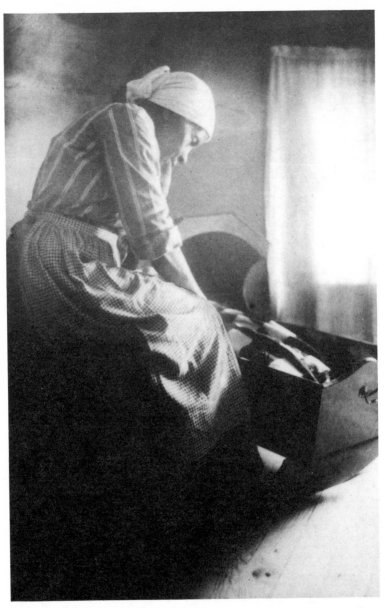

Eliza, a symphony of checks and stripes, rocks Catherine Hayden, the author's sister, in her cradle. (Courtesy of the Baltimore Museum of Art: gift of Ann Bradford Agle, daughter of Emily and Charles S. Hayden. BMA 1983.103)

Anna Bradford Hayden, Nan for short (the author), looks at the world from a safe place, Eliza's shoulder, at the age of four months—about 1905. (Courtesy of the Maryland Historical Society)

Eliza holds on to the author's sister Catherine, a pretty armful—
about 1908. (Courtesy of the Maryland Historical Society)

Eliza inspecting a new camera

"Eliza was standing beside the long wooden table sifting flour into a yellow mixing bowl, and I was close by sitting on the bottom step of the backstairs, hot tears rolling down my plump cheeks."

Eliza making muffins for supper

Anna Bradford Hayden
(the author) helping
Eliza shuck corn

The promise is kept.

A.C. BRADFORD SPENCER
1841 ——— 1882
EDWARD SPENCER
1834 ——— 1883
ELIZA BENSON
1836 ——— 1921

Putting Down New Roots

Lost my needle
Yes, ma'am
Shiny bright needle
Yes, ma'am
Hep me to find it
Yes, ma'am.

Miss Nellie, sitting in the rocker by the window where the light was best, her feet nowhere near the floor, couldn't get enough. "More, more!" she said as soon as the song ended. When Eliza couldn't think of another song to sing, the little girl would ask, "What does the hen say, Liza?" and Eliza would answer:

"Every day I lay an egg and
Sunday I have to go barefooted
Barefooted, barefooted
Barefooted"

sounding exactly like a hen who had just laid an egg.

Sewing was not all entertainment, for Miss Em had an eagle eye. Seams must be strong and neat. Darns that were not just so must be picked out stitch by stitch and done a second time. The girls soon learned it paid to do a job right the first time.

Cousin Willie taught the big girls to saddle a horse right, buckling the belly strap tight enough to keep the saddle from slipping, but not too tight. He taught them to hitch up the buggy, to cool down a horse after a run, when to water him, and when not.

Nobody had to teach anybody how to feed chickens. All you had to do was call, "Here chick, chick, chick," and when they came running with wings out, toss cracked corn out the way Boon sowed rye.

Nobody had to teach anybody how to pick berries, either. The unspoken rule was two berries dropped into the bucket to one popped into the mouth, and whoever talked the most picked the least. Picking berries could be painful, though, because thorns would grab and not let go.

Sunday everybody went to church in the carriage. Cousin Willie drove, looking sharp in gray trousers, black tail coat, white silk cravat, top hat, and dove-colored gloves. Miss Em, dressed in plum silk that rustled and poised with her back straight and head held high, was a match for him.

The girls rode in the back, Miss Nellie in the middle so she wouldn't fall out when the carriage rounded a curve at a fast clip. All three wore full skirts, bonnets tied under the chin, white stockings and black slippers. Because they were dressed up and it was Sunday, they stayed prim and proper the whole two miles.

Once they reached church, Cousin Willie tied Fleet where he could visit with the other horses. Then he helped Miss Em and the girls down.

"Good morning, Mrs. Denny."

"Good morning, Mrs. Harrison. You are looking well."

The family entered church, walked sedately down the aisle, and filled the third pew on the left. The pew in front, the Clay's Hope pew, was empty.

Eliza liked to pray. To her, God was the Good Master, a little better than Marse Bradford, bound to be, and quite like him in appearance. Praying to Him made her feel close to her people, white and black, living and dead. She asked God to bless each one and she named them, a long list starting with Miss Braddie

66

and ending with her own family: Mable, Tom, Rosa, Viney, Jonas, Marnie, Lilly, Jake, Dan, Bea, Tommie, Gabe, Steve, Paul, Annie, the twins Joe and Josie, and last of all Emily. She'd never seen Annie, the twins, and Emily, but God had. He saw everybody, so the Bible said. Miss Braddie read the Bible to her now, and fine sounding words they were to her ears. Eliza wished Mable could hear her read.

During the sermon Miss Nellie usually took a nap. Not always, though. Some Sundays she fidgeted and had to be tapped on the knee. One Sunday Miss Braddie dropped her prayer book, and Miss Nellie giggled out loud. Eliza wanted to but didn't.

Going home was lots of fun. Fleet, who found the sermon long also, stepped out fast, his mind on the pasture. The girls swayed from side to side, bumping Miss Nellie in the middle and singing lustily, "Children of the heavenly King, as ye journey sweetly sing."

Home again, Eliza was first to jump down. She ran around the house to the kitchen untying her bonnet strings so she'd be ready to help Hannah serve dinner. Being needed was important.

Days went by swiftly. It was Sunday, and before Eliza knew it, here it was Sunday again. Weeks went by and seasons. Wild geese landed on the water, spent the winter, then took off when spring came again, heading north. A year gone by, another here and gone.

The girls grew up fast, Miss Braddie the fastest. Ten years old, she was taller than fourteen-year-old Eliza. She walked like nobody else except herself—a sight worth seeing, Eliza thought—and the way she talked, you'd think for sure it was Miss Em, using big words and knowing what they meant. Eliza wished Marse

Bradford could hear her. He'd be proud too. Miss Braddie's cheeks were pink now, and she was strong and well with no sign left of being frail. She was ready to go to school in town, and Nellie was ready for first grade. Both girls would go that fall.

Eliza would not go. There was no school nearby for black girls and boys her age. Primary grades one, two, and three, yes, but not for her age. Soon there would be, within the next few years, but not then, so Miss Em said.

Looking back, Eliza enjoyed recalling August 22 of that year. "Some days drift off foggy. Dat day shine clear as a spring."

10

Miss Em's Cousin Edward

That day, August 22, Eliza and Hannah were making so much noise talking and rattling dishes after supper that they didn't know anybody was at the door until Miss Em told them. Right away Eliza dropped her tea towel, untied her kitchen apron, tied on a fresh white one, put a white cap on her head, and hurried into the house and down the hall to open the front door.

"Good evening," said the short, stocky young man standing there, a young man about sixteen or seventeen, Eliza guessed.

"Good evenin'," she said, stepping back to make way for him to come in.

"Who is there, Eliza?" Miss Em called from the living room.

"Edward Spencer, Cousin Em," the young man answered, crossing the hall with assurance.

Before returning to the kitchen, Eliza caught a glimpse of Miss Braddie sitting prim and proper beside the fireplace in the living room, her sleek head bent over her crocheting hands, her feet close together.

Eliza says she saw Miss Braddie glance up at the

visitor, say a polite "How do you do," when introduced to him, then go back to work.

As soon as Eliza walked into the kitchen, Hannah wanted to know who the visitor was and all about him.

"He a Spencer, so he say, an' he got de Spencer look, dark an' sort a bug-eyed. He got de Spencer ways, too, sure of himself as a spring frog," Eliza told her.

"He kin to our folks?" Hannah asked, and Eliza answered, "Mus' be, him callin' Miss Em cousin, an' her tellin' me to take his bag up to de guest room, which I do, an' it weigh a ton. How he related, I don't know yet. Miss Braddie set me straight later on, I speck."

Eliza was right about that. While she was brushing Miss Braddie's hair getting her ready for bed, Miss Braddie talked and talked. "He is Em's cousin on her mother's side, Liza, no blood kin to me at all. His father and my sister Em's mother, who was Eleanor Spencer, were brother and sister. And, Liza, wait 'til you hear this. His father, another Edward by the way, has another brother and guess who he is?"

Eliza didn't have a notion.

"Our minister, Dr. Joseph Spencer, D. D., our own Cousin Joe. He's why Edward is here."

"How come?" asked Eliza, making a straight part down the middle of Miss Braddie's head with the end of the comb. "What Cousin Joe got to do wid it?"

Miss Braddie jumped to her feet and began to stride up and down the bedroom floor, her long nightgown swinging. "I'm Edward addressing Em and Cousin Willie, Liza." She crossed the room taking man-sized strides, Eliza chuckling with anticipation, for Miss Braddie was a natural born mimic, enough to make you die laughing. "Better get on wid de show, Miss Em catch us still up she read de riot act."

Miss Em's Cousin Edward

In a deep voice like the visitor's Miss Braddie began: "Uncle Joseph Spencer is going to prepare me for Princeton. Studies begin at once. I planned to stay with Cousin Henry Harrison, but as you insist, I'll stay here instead. Before I left home, my mother insisted that I show you this." Miss Braddie dissolved into laughter saying, "Oh, Liza, I wish you'd been there. He had his report card from the school he'd been going to, and it really is a scream. While he was talking politics with Cousin Willie of all things, and Liza the way he talks you'd think he was at least twenty years old—anyway, while he talked I hastily jotted down some of the report card to show you. Not all, but enough so you'd know what kind of person he is."

She ran to the bureau, rummaged around in her sewing box, and found a folded piece of paper. Pulling the lamp closer, she unfolded the paper and read aloud: "Trinity School, Baltimore, Maryland, July 1850. Mrs. Spencer, Madam, I take the liberty of sending you a statement of the standing of your son, Master Edward: Latin—progress so satisfactory he can enter any college; Greek—not as advanced as Latin; French—high progress; Mathematics—satisfactory; English and Geography—few his superior; Spelling—none better; Writing, Mythology, History, Philosophy, Chemistry—excellent."

She looked up, her eyes merry. "Listen to this. He has industry and perseverance in a high degree. Halos, please. Honestly, Liza, can you imagine anybody being so la, la, la perfect? He must be dreadfully stuffy."

"I hear tell from Rosa an' 'em dat Marse Bradford, your father, know pretty near everything an' he wasn't stuffy," Eliza said. "Rosa an' Mable an' dem say when he talk, de flies stop buzzin' to listen."

71

A Promise is to Keep

There was a tap on the door and Miss Em sailed in ready for bed, sprigged wrapper billowing around her, black snake plait down her back. "To bed, both of you. It's late."

"I haven't read the Bible to Liza yet," Miss Braddie said. Miss Em was quick to reply, "Skip it tonight; recite a psalm instead." She turned down the wick of the lamp, blew out the flame, and left the room, closing the door after her.

Miss Braddie climbed into the high double bed that stood between the bureau and the dressing table, and Eliza slipped into the single bed behind the modesty screen in the corner.

"How about the Twenty-third Psalm?" Miss Braddie said. "You recite it with me, Liza, and don't mumble, speak out." Together in the dark they recited reverently the beautiful, familiar words: "The Lord is my shepherd, I shall not want. He maketh me to lie down in green pastures ..."

For a moment after the recitation, Eliza savored her favorite line, "my cup runneth over." Then both girls hopped out of bed, knelt down, said a quick prayer, and hopped back. Shortly Miss Braddie said, "School starts next Tuesday, and I can hardly wait. You can see us off, Liza, and as soon as I get home I'll tell you everything that happens all day."

"Don't you worry 'bout me. I got things to do myself."

"I know. Good night."

"Good night, Miss Braddie, see you in de mornin'."

After a while Miss Braddie said, "Liza, I forgot to tell you he'll walk to St. Michaels with us every day. He'll go to 'Solitude,' where Cousin Joe lives, and I'll go to school not far away. That will be a mile and a half of silence except for Nellie and me chattering."

"Who you talkin' 'bout an' how come all dat silence?"

"Edward Spencer. I'll never be able to think of a thing to say to him. If I did, I'd never be able to say it, old and learned and full of industry and perseverance as he is."

Eliza chuckled. "Ask him how he related to Miss Em's mother, ol' Miss Spencer. Time he get through de fam'ly you be at de school house door. Go to sleep now, honey, so you kin wake up full of industry an' percy-verence."

Miss Braddie sat up in bed. "Are you teasing me, Eliza Ann?"

"No indeedy, no indeedy."

"No indeedy, no indeedy," Miss Braddie mimicked. If they'd been outdoors, she would have chased Eliza across the lawn and around the black walnut tree three times, maybe four. Eliza knew it—and laughed again. She and Miss Braddie had so much fun together.

Even so, with a guest in the guest room, for no telling how long, she'd have plenty of extra work to do. Work was the best thing in the world, so Rosa said, and Rosa knew.

11

School Days,
One Kind and Another

Tuesday morning of the following week Eliza stood in the dusty road in front of the Mount Pleasant gate. Shielding her eyes with her hand, she watched the other children on their way to school, Edward Spencer and his cousin Henry Harrison on ahead of the girls. It was time for Miss Braddie to go to school. With her whole heart, Eliza was glad to see her go. When she told me about seeing Miss Braddie and the others walking out of sight, I asked her if she minded being left behind. She said: "What was bes' fer Miss Braddie was bes' fer me. Besides, I had things to study myself."

At the end of the road, Miss Braddie turned around and waved, and Eliza, so she said, waved back. Then she walked quickly up the driveway, around the house, and into the kitchen. She and Hannah had the day planned. They were going to start fall housecleaning. School was one kind of work; house cleaning was another. Both were honorable, so Rosa said. Rosa claimed all work was honorable. Eliza said that once back in Clay's Hope days she had balked at carrying a slop jar out to the necessary house and Rosa had scolded her. "What got to be done in dis world got to be done and the Good Lord know it." Rosa was a fine teacher. Marse Bradford was too, and so were Mable and Tom. For sure Miss Em was. "You mine Miss Em, you end up knowin' plenty."

"Where Hannah?" Eliza asked Boon as she tied on her work apron.

"She in de dinin' room a'ready. She say tell you she dere."

By the time it took to say Jack Robinson, Eliza was there herself, standing on a kitchen chair so she could reach the top shelf of the china closet.

"Here, Hannah. Set dis tureen on de table an' mine how you drop it. Dat de ticket. An' han' me de dust brush an' fetch me a basin a water, some soap, an' a dryin' cloth," she ordered.

"Yes, ma'am, Miss Benson," Hannah answered. "Nobody told me you was de lady of de house."

Eliza laughed so hard her dust cap fell down over her eyes. "I speck I do soun' bossy, givin' orders faster dan Miss Em. I got things pressin' on my min' is why. First time Miss Braddie been away from me ever. It bound to sting some. Work tend to de sting. Here, take dis pitcher an' watch out how you dus' off de hannel."

They both laughed at that so loud Miss Em came to the door to find out what was going on.

Fun made time go by fast. Before Eliza knew it, the hall clock struck lunch time, and the next thing she knew it struck coming-home-from-school time. As Eliza opened the door for the girls, Master Edward nowhere in sight, she said, "Sun bonnets off! Go 'round wid your faces mother-naked, you look like a couple a speckled turkey eggs come spring. An' look at your shoes. Stand right dere on de door mat 'til I brush off de dust."

During the dust-off, Miss Braddie talked fast. "Fifteen girls in my class, Liza, all of them real nice. Our teacher Mr. Martin is nice too. I wish you could see him—tall, thin, and looks like a crane with glasses on. He's funny, too, not meaning to be. It's the way he clears his throat and says a-hem."

Shoes dusted, the girls followed Eliza to the kitchen for cambric tea and bread-and-butter-and-brown sugar. "I was wrong about Edward, Liza. He's not a bit stuffy. He isn't, is he, Nellie?"

Nellie agreed he was not a single bit. Back in the kitchen over tea, Miss Braddie kept on about Edward Spencer. "He won't be home until supper time I guess. He has so much to cover in a short time, he'll be studying night and day, Liza. Walking along, he conversed with us as though we were highly intelligent, mature people, which of course we are, a-hem, a-hem. He believes passionately in state's rights the way Jefferson did, or was it Alexander Hamilton?"

Eliza, not up on politics, changed the subject. "You get butter on dat new dress, Miss Em throw a conniption fit." Back to the subject of school, she added, "Soun' to me like school start at de front gate." Chewing away, both girls nodded agreement.

Rainy days, cold days, and very hot days, Boon drove the young people to school in the buggy and fetched them home again. Every day, rain or shine, as soon as she was out of earshot of anyone else, Miss Braddie brought Eliza up to date on events of the day and what Edward said.

"He's a walking encyclopedia, Liza. Mention any

subject: politics, plays, poetry, books, philosophy, anything—and he's off. Today on the way home he told us about the death of President Taylor, Millard Fillmore being president next. After that, he was saying how the Texas boundary was finally settled. Then he got so excited over the new fugitive slave law, I thought he was going to burst. He didn't, though, just cooled himself down by reciting a new poem by Whittier, just published. And, Nellie, who was it he said influenced Emerson?"

"Plato. Or maybe it was Amelia Bloomer," the little girl answered.

Miss Braddie roared with laughter at that. "Emerson would collapse if he heard you say that, Nellie. Mrs. Bloomer is the woman who has been promoting the screamingly funny full pants gathered at the ankle."

It was Nellie who told Eliza that Edward carried Miss Braddie's books, adding in a stage whisper, "And sometimes the two of them walk along hand in hand." Liza didn't need to be told. She had seen the two young people come through the gate and she had seen them walking down along the river.

Time flew—winter, then summer again—and the next fall Miss Braddie was off to boarding school in Wilmington, Delaware. There was no use looking down the road at four o'clock because nobody would be scuffing up the dust. Not a soul. Miss Braddie gone, Master Edward at Princeton, Master Henry Harrison somewhere else, Eliza didn't know just where. Miss Nellie still went to school in St. Michaels, but she was the only one to go from nearby. Boon or her father and Fleet took her every day in the buggy and brought her home.

A Promise is to Keep

With Miss Braddie gone, Eliza did the only thing she could do. She lived one day at a time and made the best of it. She had to. She worked hard, learning from her teacher Miss Em everything a well-trained servant should know, so Miss Em said. In her spare time she played games with Miss Nellie, who followed her around upstairs and down. In the kitchen she picked up cooking tricks from Delia, the cook. Delia, Boon's wife, a tall, thin woman from Jamaica, was a gifted cook. "Her terrapin dishes made you smack your lips an' ask fer more," Eliza, a gifted cook herself, told me years later. Delia's crab cakes were delicious; she had the lightest hand at patting oysters Eliza had ever seen. And she had seen plenty of oyster patting. Delia's biscuits were light, too. The crown went to Hannah for Maryland beaten biscuits, though. Pounded with an ax, they were in a class by themselves.

Watching those two, Delia and Hannah, listening to them, asking questions, Eliza learned some valuable cooking secrets: a touch of nutmeg on roast of beef, honey instead of sugar in applesauce, never let biscuit dough leave your hand—things like that.

Thanksgiving day, Delia let Eliza stuff the turkey. Hannah made the dressing, and Eliza helped serve. It should have been a gala day, the table looked so pretty, with the best china, napkins white as snow, glasses sparkling, and dinner excellent from terrapin soup to pumpkin pie. But it was not gala because Miss Braddie was not there. At the last minute she changed her mind and went to her sister Mary's in Philadelphia. Eliza served dinner with a set jaw.

The day after Thanksgiving there was a knock on the front door and who should be doing the knocking but Viney.

School Days, One Kind and Another

"What in de name a peace you doin' knockin' on de front door, Viney Benson?" Eliza said, opening the door wide enough for the cat to slide in and no wider. "Go 'round to de back door where you belong an' I'll let you in."

"All dis time go by an' dat's de welcome I gits," Viney said, flouncing off the step. Once the sisters met in the kitchen, the welcome was warm as a midsummer day. They embraced, wept a little, backed off, then embraced again, each saying how fine the other looked. As soon as the hugging tapered off, Eliza served tea, and Viney asked over the second cup how would Eliza like to go with her to town to visit Mable and Tom. Eliza would indeed if Miss Em were willing.

Miss Em was more than willing. She told her to forget Miss Braddie and have a carefree, good time. Forget Miss Braddie? It was well-seen Miss Em didn't know Eliza. As soon as Eliza changed into her Sunday dress, she and Viney set off for St. Michaels, walking fast and talking faster. For a half mile Viney put on airs, telling her sister about being a high-flying French cook up in Baltimore. Finally she settled down to being herself and talked about the old days at Clay's Hope and their own people, black and white.

To their disappointment, nobody was home at the little two-story house on Second Street, one block from the wharf. They knocked, waited awhile, and then, as the door was unlocked, went in. Right away they felt at home, seeing so many familiar things there. The mirror over the stove Miss Mary had given to Mable one Christmas; the worn rug in the front room belonged to ol' Miss El'ner years ago; the pie crust table used to be Miss Em's; and every single patch in the patchwork quilt was an old friend.

A Promise is to Keep

The house was neat and clean. "Not a speck a dus'," Viney said, running a lean finger across the back of the rocker that used to be in the sewing room at Clay's Hope.

"They both at work somewheres, I speck," Viney said. "We come again. Let's go, Eliza Ann. Let's us go befo' I git homesick."

The sisters left the house and walked down toward the wharf to see if the mail boat was in. It was, and never had Eliza's eyes rested on anything as splendid as that steam packet. Nothing would ever make her set foot on it with all that water underneath, still it was easy on the eyes.

Viney's eyes were on the men loading the packet. "Um-ump," she said, swishing her narrow hips. "Um-ump." Eliza thought to herself that Viney was a caution, she really was. Back home at Mount Pleasant, Eliza told Miss Em that although she was sorry to miss seeing her parents, she did so enjoy the day with Viney.

"She citified, not due to be free for a while yet, but her spirit free aready. She put me in mind a Master Edward Spencer. Miss Em, nobody seen hide nor hair a him in a coon's age. What you speck he up to?"

"Cousin Joe keeps in touch with him, Eliza. According to him, Edward is making a name for himself at Princeton with his writing. He'll show up one of these days."

He didn't show up for years, not until Miss Braddie had graduated from finishing school. She was nineteen then, tall, slender, and pretty enough to stop a runaway horse, so Eliza said. Miss Braddie and two of her friends had spent the day in town sewing at church.

"Liza, guess who I met today?" she said as she came in the house, even before she hung up her bonnet.

80

"Cousin Joe?"

"No. Guess again."

"De President a de United States."

"Oh, Liza, no. Be serious, take one more guess."

"I give up."

"Edward Spencer. And, Liza, you should see him. He always was mature, even at seventeen. Now he's positively distinguished."

"He tall?"

"No, he's not tall, but he has a mustache that droops this way." Using both hands, Miss Braddie portrayed a magnificent droop. "He treated me as though I were a grown woman, which of course I am. He took off his hat and bowed this way."

Eliza laughed at the bow. "You both grown up since he lef' here."

"I know. Miss Em was married when she was my age."

Eliza gave her a searching look. "You not figgerin' to marry him, I hope."

Miss Braddie twirled around on her toes, arms spread wide. "Of course not. We were fond of one another when we were children and we just met again, that's all there is to it. This is the way it happened: We met face to face on the street. He said, 'How do you do, Miss Harrison?' I said, 'How do you do, Mr. Spencer?' Then he said, 'I trust your sister and her family are well.' I said, 'Yes, thank you, and I hope your mother and brothers are well.' As you know, Liza, his father died some time ago, 1839 or 40. And he said, 'Yes, thank you.' All very formal and proper. As he was leaving, he bowed again and asked if he might have permission to call Sunday afternoon and I said, 'Pray do.'"

81

A Promise is to Keep

The clear picture Miss Braddie painted of the meeting made Eliza feel as though she'd been present herself, and Eliza handed the picture on to me. "It was grand havin' Miss Braddie home, no more goin' off to school," Eliza said. Miss Braddie was happy to be home most of the time. Not all of the time, though. Not when Mr. Spencer did not come to call on Sunday. A messenger came on horseback to say that Mr. Spencer's brother Tom was ill, and he must return home at once.

Miss Braddie was sorry about Tom and sorry about Sunday.

"What you pacin' up an' down for?" Eliza asked. "How come all a sudden you got to rearrange furniture right an' lef'? Why you turn down a secon' helpin' a turtle soup an' eat only one biscuit?"

Miss Braddie didn't answer, just shrugged her shoulders.

The following Saturday the mail packet from Baltimore arrived at St. Michaels as usual. It tied up as usual, and as usual the mailbag was tossed on the dock. In the bag this time, along with business letters, bills, family letters, and official notices for residents of Talbot County, was a pale blue letter addressed to:

> Miss Braddie Harrison
> Mount Pleasant
> St. Michaels
> Maryland

12

The First Blue Letter

Eliza, on all fours in the front hall, vigorously rubbed up foot tracks with a damp cloth. As she rubbed she mumbled to herself. "Worse than a chicken run, tracks every which way." Hearing the familiar clop, clop of Fleet returning from town, she hopped up, and by the time the gig stopped at the door, she was on the step, hand reaching out for the mail.

"It's a fin' day, Eliza, after yestiddy's rain."

"Good mornin', Boon. Yes indeedy, a fin' day."

Clop, clop, Fleet went on down to the barn, and Eliza went back in the house. There were three letters today, one for Cousin Willie—a bill most likely by the looks of it—one for Miss Em from her sister Mary in Philadelphia, and one for Miss Braddie. Was it reading to know by sight the three names, the telling of Mr. from Mrs., and both from Miss? Eliza reckoned so. She turned Miss Braddie's letter over in her hand, weighing it. Pale blue it was, with an air of destiny in the fine, clear handwriting.

"Miss Braddie, a letter fer you," she called up the stairs.

A Promise is to Keep

In the time it took to take one breath, Miss Braddie sailed down the steps, swooped the letter out of Eliza's hand, sailed up again, and went into her room, and shut the door bang.

Eliza chuckled as she kneeled down to resume work. Before she had wiped up a single foot print, Miss Braddie called from the bedroom door. "Liza, come here fast. I have something very important to tell you."

After hiding the floor cloth in the umbrella stand, Eliza joined Miss Braddie in their room.

"Sit and listen," Miss Braddie said. "I'm going to read you something special."

> "I ain't got no time to play
> Chillen's way.
> I got this here chile to mind
> I got this here quilt to bind
> I ain't got no time to play
> Chillen's way."

recited Eliza, and Miss Braddie said, "Mable's poem, Rosa's too. I'm glad you recited it now because my letter is a poem. It really is, Liza, a poem by Edward Spencer to me. Listen, I'll read it to you and don't you dare giggle because it is *not* funny. It is beautiful. Promise me you won't laugh."

Eliza nodded her head. "Promise ef it chokes me not to. Read away. I'm alistenin' only hurry it up. I got work to do. Like I tell you, I ain't got no time to play, chillen's way."

"I am not a child," was the quick reply. "Now the poem: 'The Meeting' by Edward Spencer:

84

The First Blue Letter

"She came down the street and I
vow that her bonnet
Deserved all a lover's invections
upon it,
For 'twas so much enveloped in
ribbon and lace
One sought all in vain for a
glimpse of her face."

"The 'her' is me, Eliza, as you'll soon see.

"She came down the street, the
center of three—
What would you have done, had
you only been me?
Have passed her or kissed her or
dropped on your knees?
I give you my word, sir, I did
none of these."

"Sound mighty fine," Eliza said, starting for the door.
"Put me in mind a Shakespeare an' de Bible."

"Wait," said Miss Braddie, blocking the way. "There
are two more verses. Ready?"

Eliza folded her arms, nodding, and Miss Braddie
read on:

"There were frogs in my throat
but I held out my hand
The veil hid her eyes—she said a
word—and
Then I bowed and moved on, and
on she moved, too

A Promise is to Keep

She labeled me 'Mister' and I
called her 'You.'

"But oh the new friend thus
made on the street
Is all I have dreamed of, and ten
times more sweet;
She has showered upon me the
wealth of her grace
And I see my own heart when I
look in her face.

"It's beautiful, isn't it, Eliza?"

Eliza agreed it was and added, "Seem he takin' a round about way sayin' he glad to see you. I got to hurry now. I hear Miss Em stirrin' downstairs. She find my floor cloth, she wallop de stuffins out a me."

"She would not and you know it. She might want to, be angry enough to, but she never would. Liza, don't tell her about the poem or Cousin Willie. Or Nellie or anybody. I don't want to be teased about anything as sacred as a poem."

Eliza promised, a cloud passing over her. Hand on the door knob, she turned to face Miss Braddie and warned her not to go whole hog over Mister Spencer. "I know he kin to ol' Miss Spencer," she said. "Even so, bes' take it a step at a time 'til you know him better."

"What do you mean 'know him better'? I've known him since we were children. You know that. You know we walked home from school hand in hand and played games together after supper. You know he carried my books day after day and was a close, dear friend when he was a boy."

The First Blue Letter

"Boy one thing. Grown man somethin' else altogether diff'rent."

Miss Braddie frowned. "Cousin Joe Spencer speaks well of him. He told Cousin Willie that Edward has a well-trained mind, shows promise, and will go far."

"Far sometimes go both ways," Eliza told her. "What Cousin Joe say is front door news. Back door news not dat high falutin'."

Miss Braddie stiffened her back. "I presume you are referring to the fact that Edward is poor. Well, he is and with good reason. His father left plenty of money to take care of his family, but his mother, out of the kindness of her heart, foolishly lent nearly all of it to relatives and friends. Now, with hardly enough to live on, she and her sons run The Martin's Nest, a farm in Randallstown, or try to anyway. No matter what people say, poverty is not a disgrace."

"No," agreed Eliza. "De rumor goin' round, it 'bout somethin' else altogether diff'rent from bein' poor."

Miss Braddie burst into tears and pushed Eliza out of the room. "You are horrid to imply base things about him. I'm sorry I read the poem to you. Go away and leave me alone."

Eliza, her feelings hurt, hurried down the steps. By the time she reached the front hall, Miss Braddie was there too, begging to be forgiven. "I didn't mean what I said, Liza. Forgive me and tell me what you heard about Edward. I must know."

Eliza drew away from her. "Ask Miss Em an' Cousin Willie. They tell you. De Lord strike me dead if I speak a word against a kin a Marse Bradford. Own brother or his wife's second cousin, all de same. Kin is kin. Ask Miss Em an' dem."

A Promise is to Keep

Miss Braddie lost no time. She confronted Miss Em in the sewing room and Cousin Willie down on the dock, and both said the same thing. Edward Spencer was considered wild at college. He drank heavily, and his name had been linked with that of a city woman.

Miss Braddie relayed the rumors to Eliza. "I do not believe a word of it, and until Edward himself confirms the accusations, which I am sure he won't, I shall continue to have faith in his purity and innocence. To me he is . . . he is . . . I can't put him in words. All I know is I am my best self because of him."

"You feel dat way 'bout him he boun' to be a fin' man," Eliza said.

Miss Braddie responded, "He is and I intend to forget I ever heard anything to the contrary." She grabbed Eliza's hand. "Let's go see the new calf. Boon says it is adorable. Well, he didn't actually say that, but from what he did say, I'm sure it is. Come on."

Eliza declared she was too busy to go, but Miss Nellie wasn't. So the two girls walked down to the barn, Miss Braddie chattering about nothing much, trying to push back the gray rumor. The calf helped, for it really was adorable, with great big soft-brown eyes and the longest eyelashes.

Back at the house again, Nellie helped Eliza shell peas while Miss Braddie played the piano. She attacked the keys with such vigor that Hannah said to Eliza, "What come over her? She hittin' white keys an' black wif bof hans ten fer Sunday like she callin' up de saints."

Eliza didn't answer, but she knew. Miss Braddie was in love for better or worse. "Lord, let it be for better," she prayed, hands resting on pea hulls in her lap, head bowed.

13

A Few Visits and a Whole Lot of Letters

Three Sundays went by before Mister Edward Spencer paid a call on Miss Braddie Harrison. The way Miss Braddie had been moping around the house, Eliza was mighty glad to see him. After tea with the family, the two young people took a walk. From the kitchen window, Eliza watched them cross the lawn talking together and then go down along the shore path. As Miss Braddie was a great one for clearing the air as soon as possible, Eliza felt sure she'd face him with the unsavory rumors before returning to the house.

He didn't stay to supper. Miss Braddie shut herself in her room and refused to come to the table—bad signs, Eliza thought to herself. Miss Em must have thought so, too, for she told Eliza to leave Miss Braddie alone, not even take a tray to her.

"Yes, Miss Em," Eliza said. "Oyster stew, beaten biscuits, an' blackberry flummery . . . seem a shame though."

The next morning Miss Braddie, red rings around her eyes, dark circles under them, announced that the rumors were true. She did not forgive him, could not, would not if she could; so that was that. It took Edward forty-seven pale blue letters, prose, neatly written and long, plus two face-to-face visits at Mount Pleasant to convince Miss Braddie that his shortcomings were past history, over and done with for good.

Letter number fifty-four, in which he said, "I may disappoint you, dearest Braddie, but I will never betray you," thawed the ice. When Eliza heard what he'd said, she gave him highest praise. "Soun' like Marse Bradford talkin'." Her favorite letter was about when he was born. She made Miss Braddie read it aloud over and over again.

Night after night she said, "Read it again, Miss Braddie," and before the lamp was blown out, Miss Braddie sat up in bed and read.

"June 23, 1834—my birthday—Do you know that I was an unusually pretty baby? My nose was not so big as now, my hair was jet black, long and was parted in the middle at my birth. I was larger than common— very fat and plump—had rosy cheeks, and my eyes were black and sparkling like dewberries in milk. Mammy Toole, who officiated on the occasion, told me that I have never been as pretty since. I didn't cry, took everything as a matter of course, and accommodated myself to the singular change in my circumstances with that apt facility that has ever been my distinguishing characteristic."

Once trust had been established between them, Edward and Braddie announced their engagement. Then letters poured in and kept on pouring in, arriving on every packet. Writing letters when he was engaged was easy. The next step took money, and Edward didn't have any. Pay for stories printed in *The Baltimore*

Weekly Sun and *The Southern Magazine* amounted to little more than enough to mend the plow and buy a few books.

Money or no money, Miss Braddie floated on air. Miss Nellie, a born romantic, floated with her. Eliza hummed as she washed dishes, her mind aglow with thoughts of filling the hope chest and making clothes for the bride. How fine everything was going to be living at The Martin's Nest, the three of them: Miss Braddie, Marse Edward, and of course Eliza. Where Miss Braddie lived was home.

Miss Em was not enthusiastic about her sister's engagement. She liked Edward well enough and was reasonably sure he'd straightened himself out but she did not like his politics. He had been an anti-slave Whig until the party, what was left of it, became the Republican Party. Then he joined the anti-slavery Democrats. He stumped for the cause loudly in Randallstown, in Baltimore, and at the dinner table, claiming that each state had the right to decide its own domestic problems without interference from any other state or from the federal government.

Although Miss Em and Cousin Willie considered themselves to be Southerners, they were also loyal supporters of the Union. That year, 1860, had no middle ground. The enemy was where you found him—across town, across the creek, across the dining room table. And Edward was an out-and-out, fire-eating rebel.

The Baltimore papers, the New York papers, the *Gazette,* and the *Easton Star* carried news of the burning split in the country between state sovereignty and nationalism. Southern states led by South Carolina, sure of their beliefs, formed The Confederacy, seceded from the Union, drew up their own constitution, and elected Jefferson Davis president—Georgia, Florida, Alabama, Mississippi, Arkansas, Louisiana, and Texas. To rebel Edward Spencer's fury, Maryland was not included. Many Marylanders shared his viewpoint, though not enough to swing the balance their way.

Times were not good for a struggling, young, Southern journalist for the literary market was in the North. Although *Harper's* and *The Atlantic* printed several of Edward Spencer's stories, most of them landed in his desk drawer. Luckily he had an eager market for his letters, Miss Braddie. Two, sometimes three a week, came down from Baltimore on the mail packet.

The letters kept Miss Braddie and Eliza up to date on local news and news across the country. The South had cotton, tobacco, rice, and sugar cane planted and harvested by slave labor. Poor whites, unable to find work, grew poorer still in the North as well as in the South. North-imported foreign help was cheaper than domestic or slave labor. In the South, industry was stunted from lack of banking capital, lack of technological skill, and lack of equipment, though there was plenty of iron, coal, and timber. Both North and South had a purpose: one to maintain the Union, the other to maintain the independent slave-owning Confederacy.

Not all of Edward's letters were political. Listening to Miss Braddie reading aloud a vivid description of the farm at Randallstown, Eliza could see clearly the chickens pecking corn, looking up, pecking again. She could hear them talking chicken talk and hear the cow lowing for her calf in the adjoining field at weaning time. She liked the way Marse Edward spoke of his mother with affection, humor, and respect.

Then came a letter full of sorrow. Edward's younger brother Tom died. Too young to die, the much-loved young man, weakened by a long and painful struggle with the dreaded consumption, coughed himself to death in Edward's arms. The letter telling about the death was a sharp cry of caring, a deep racking sob of grief. Miss Braddie could hardly read it for weeping, and Eliza wept inwardly for Master Tom, Marse Edward, Miss Braddie, and herself. Bound together they were now.

So much was happening to the country that personal sorrow had to be set aside. Letters, some illustrated by Edward himself, were full of news—about how South Carolina, objecting to interference from the federal government, asked President Buchanan to remove troops from the Charleston Harbor. He refused and sent supplies to the fort. On and on the letters went, telling how South Carolina fired on the supply ship and again demanded removal of federal troops from Fort Sumter. How the President, not willing to alienate the foreign market—tobacco and cotton mostly—did nothing, preferring to pass the buck to the President-elect Abraham Lincoln.

Mr. Lincoln, born in Kentucky, was a speech-making lawyer, as Edward said, a senator from Illinois, where he had set up his practice. On the way to Washington from Springfield, he made speeches, short and to the point, to back up his Republican and Union stand. Warned of a plot to assassinate him in Baltimore, he side-stepped that city and took the night train secretly to Washington.

A Promise is to Keep

On March 4, President Lincoln assured the South that it would be protected—that he had no purpose to interfere with the institution of slavery in states where it already existed. On the other hand, secession would not be tolerated. "We cannot separate." He'd reached the White House, won the election on the strength of his character and the strength of his "a house divided will fall."

One of President Lincoln's first decisions was to send more supplies to Fort Sumter. South Carolina, fearing a long federal occupation, requested Major Anderson, commander of the fort, to surrender. Knowing supplies were on the way, he refused. Shore guns fired on the fort and the bloody, cruel Civil War began. What does the war have to do with Eliza's life? That year everybody's life hung on a thin political thread.

Major Anderson surrendered. Shortly after that the border states, Virginia, Tennessee, and North Carolina, joined the Confederacy. Kentucky remained neutral. Cousin Willie joined the Maryland Militia, a Captain he was and proud to be, brother Jonathan joined a Texas unit, and Edward's brother Bob joined the Confederate Army of Northern Virginia. Edward, turned down because of poor eyesight, patrolled the road near his home out of uniform, his own gun over his shoulder. When not on duty, he wrote fierce editorials for the Baltimore papers until they were placed under military censorship. Then he contributed to the *Copper-head Newark Evening Journal*.

With determination and passion he worked himself into a "skinny rednose" on the farm by day, long hours of writing at night. Toward dawn he wrote to Braddie. He missed her so much, the missing was a sickness. He had to see her and set the date for the wedding. War or no war, he could no longer live without her.

So, dropping plow and pen, he boarded the steamer to spend the weekend at Mount Pleasant. The visit was not a success. Oh, the part with Braddie was perfect, but he crossed swords with Miss Em again. This time he overstepped the margin of good manners and so did Miss Em. He left in a hurry, Eliza saying as she closed the door after him, "If Cousin Willie were home where he belongs he could patch things up." Miss Braddie answered, "Not this time, Eliza."

Back home he wrote: "I left town Tuesday night on foot, having missed the omnibus and being forced to go to keep out of jail. I saw enough of the outrageous occupation of Baltimore, of the infamous disregard of property and person to provoke me beyond reason. I was four times arrested . . . bade folks good-by and started on foot. The troops quartered in Baltimore are the merest rabble, insolent blackguards. I know of outrages committed by the scoundrels that I cannot repeat to you. Oh, how I wished for ten thousand good and true men. I would have been that night in Fort McHenry or in my grave." Reading aloud, Miss Braddie looked up and said, "It's pages and pages longer, but that's enough to give you a gist of things, Liza."

Eliza was darning the toe of a white stocking. "Put Marse Edward 'longside Mr. Robert E. Lee, de war be over in no time."

Miss Braddie answered, "General Lee will lead the Confederate Army to victory, you'll see. He's such a fine man, such a splendid general, he's bound to win." Wistfully she added, "Edward is fine, too. Poor Edward, he cares so much about his country, about Maryland, and me."

One form of caring arrived by mail, a poem called "Birds at my Window." Eliza liked it very much.

> Sweet birds that by my window
>   sing
> Or sail around on careless wing
> Beseech ye lend your caroling
> While I salute my darling.

There were eight verses, and Eliza liked them all. As the poem was published, she was not the only one who did. Of course, Miss Braddie liked it. While she and Eliza sewed on her trousseau, she memorized all eight verses and recited them to Eliza until she knew most of them, too.

> She's far from me, away, away,
> Beyond the hills, beyond the bay,
> But still my heart goes night and
>   day,
>   To meet and greet my darling.
> Brown wren from out whose
>   swelling throat
> Unstinted joys of music float,
> Come, lend to me thy own June
>   note
>   To warble to my darling.
> Sweet dove they tender, lovelorn
>   coo,
> Melts pensively the orchard
>   through,

A Few Visits and a Whole Lot of Letters

Grant me thy gentle voice to
    woo,
  And I shall win my darling.
Lark ever leal to dawn of day,
Pause e're thou wingst thy sky-
    ward way,
Pause and bestow one quivering
    lay,
  One anthem for my darling.
Oh mocker, rich in leafy June,
Thou'lt grant, I know, a little
    boon,
One strain of thy most matchless
    tune,
  To solace my own darling.
Bright choir, your peerless song
    will stir,
The rapturous chords of love in
    her;
And who shall be our messenger,
  When we salute my darling?
Oh voiceless swallow, crown of
    spring,
Lend me awhile thy swift curved
    wing:
Straight as an arrow thou shalt
    bring,
  This greeting to my darling.

Edward Spencer, June 27, 1861

Edward was not alone in feeling keenly the long separation.

A Promise is to Keep

Finally the date for the wedding was set—November 25, 1861. Edward declared he could not return to Talbot County and Miss Em. Not yet. The marriage would take place at 753 South Ninth Street, Philadelphia, home of Braddie's sister Mary, her husband The Reverend Ruth officiating. Miss Em gave her blessing coolly, but she would not attend, thank you. Eliza heard her say, "How could Miss Braddie go off someplace else to be married after all Cousin Willie and I have done for her?"

Whether the wedding was to be at St. Michaels or Philadelphia, Eliza was glad everything was settled at last. Miss Braddie's clothes were ready: a plum dress, double skirt with puff sleeves trimmed in bands of velvet, and a velvet basque with three rows of lace at the neck. The wedding dress was a tan satin, the low neck edged with satin cord, the same color as the dress. The long full skirt was so full and stiff it could almost stand up by itself. There was a charming plum cape, lined in navy blue to wear over a navy, wool traveling-dress, topped by a plum-colored bonnet.

Eliza was so busy packing Miss Braddie's clothes she didn't get around to packing her own until the last minute. At eight o'clock of the morning Miss Braddie was to go, the packet leaving at ten, she was putting her second best dress in her carpet bag when Miss Em came to the door.

"You are not going, Eliza," Miss Em said in a firm voice.

Eliza straightened up and looked her full in the face with unbelieving eyes. Brought up by Mable, Tom, and Rosa, she would not dare to question Miss Em. After a long silence Miss Em said, "I should have told you before. Knowing how devoted you are to my sister, I could not bring myself to mention it. I am sorry, truly sorry, Eliza. Even so, considering the fact that I have trained you over the years, made you into a valuable servant, I feel justified in keeping you here. You owe it to me to stay and work for me." She waited for Eliza to say, "Yes, ma'am," but waited in vain. Eliza said nothing.

After an icy silence Miss Em went on. "Do not speak to Braddie about the subject. When I told her last evening, she was very upset, and I do not want her to be upset again this morning. My mind is made up, Eliza."

Again, Miss Em waited in vain for Eliza's "Yes ma'am," then went on downstairs, back straight, skirt swinging as she stepped. Eliza went on packing. She felt sure that at the last minute Miss Braddie would refuse to go without her, Miss Em would give in, and all would be well.

It was time to go. Carriage at the door, Boon loaded the trousseau-filled bags in the back. Down the steps came Miss Braddie, wearing the new navy traveling dress, plum cape, and bonnet. Seeing Eliza standing by the door, she rushed over to her, threw her arms around her narrow shoulder, and sobbed. "I can't bear to leave you, Liza, and I have to. I'll come to visit you soon and often. We'll see each other. Tell me you understand."

Eliza stiffened. Without a word she walked down the hall, out the back door, into the kitchen, and on to the pantry where she hid. At ten o'clock when the paddle wheel turned and the packet pulled away from the dock, Miss Braddie was on board and Eliza was still hiding in the pantry at Mount Pleasant.

14

At the Bottom of the Well

Eliza heard the carriage come home. She heard Miss Em and Miss Nellie come in the house. She knew she should be on hand to take their wraps upstairs and put away their bonnets, but she said she couldn't. She felt turned in on herself, squinched in, an empty shell at the bottom of the well. She didn't blame Miss Braddie for leaving her. A younger sister was bound to do what her older sister said, and as the sun crossed the sky Miss Braddie had to go to Marse Edward and their wedding.

Miss Em was to blame. She was on hand when her father Marse Bradford gave Eliza to Miss Braddie. With her own ears she had heard him say what was what. From the beginning she knew Eliza Ann was not an ordinary slave. There was an advertisement in the *Easton Star* that Miss Braddie read aloud one time, so Eliza said, and she relayed it to me. "For sale, a Negro woman, good cook, washer and ironer, thirty-four years old and healthy, who has three children, one, four, and nine, all healthy and sound and slaves for life."

Well, Eliza was not for sale, never had been, and never would be. She was a Negro woman twenty-five years old, a healthy, well-trained servant, and she belonged to Miss Braddie Harrison, who in three days time would be Mrs. Edward Spencer. She did not belong to Mrs. Willie Harrison and never would.

"Liza, Liza, where are you?" Miss Nellie called from the kitchen. "Mother wants you this minute. Hurry up, she has a good idea."

Reluctantly, Eliza came out of hiding and went to the sitting room where she listened in silence to Miss Em talking fast as a trotting horse. "We'll do over the house. We'll make Nellie's room into the guest room. We'll paint the walls dusty blue, the woodwork white, make new curtains and a new bed spread."

"What about me?" asked Nellie.

"You take over Braddie's room and Eliza can move to the little room opposite Hannah's over the kitchen."

Nellie was delighted. Eliza was not and didn't expect to be until things were set to rights. Until they were, she'd live a day at a time in silence or with as few words as possible. With a heavy heart she lugged her belongings downstairs into the kitchen and up the kitchen steps. The new room was not pretty. That was all right, it was clean and warm, the heat rising up from the kitchen. She put her clothes in the narrow chest at the foot of the narrow bed and then she sat on the only chair in the narrow niche by the dormer window big enough for pigeons. Eliza told me she was not sorry for herself. She said by that time she was good and angry, and her chin jutted out in revolt.

For three days and nights Eliza went about the house in silence, doing as little work as possible and doing it half-heartedly. In the back of her head she kept trying to figure out why she was where she was instead of where she belonged. Slowly she came to the conclusion: it was because she was an excellent servant. Very well, that being true, from now on she would not be. To be slow, to do just enough and do that in a don't care manner was hard for Eliza, but she would manage. And she'd manage to keep one inch from being impudent to Miss Em. She had to. Hannah was the one to get after her first. "How come you eatin' an' not earnin' what you eat?"

Hannah told Miss Em, and Miss Em checked on Eliza and clamped down on her hard. "Look at that bed spread hanging way down on the side. Straighten it at once, Eliza. What's gotten into you? I declare you are enough to try the patience of Job," she said sharply.

One time Miss Em caught Eliza peeling potatoes at a snail's pace, cutting away more than she dropped in the iron pot. Miss Em scolded her, called her lazy and wasteful. In time, Eliza became listless and thin. Hoping to raise her spirits, Miss Em sent Boon to town one Sunday to fetch Mable and Tom. The visit was a great success. Eliza found that her parents were the same, free as they were when they were slaves. Both of them were respectful, soft-spoken, gentle, fine people. They brought back memories of Clay's Hope, of Eliza, her brothers and sisters playing together, and best of all Miss Braddie when she was a little girl. Eliza hated to see her parents leave, and as the carriage went down the driveway, she felt so lonely.

The following Sunday Eliza had another visitor, a suitor. According to her, he was a nice-looking young man, free, with a plot of land of his own, a mule, and a garden already tilled waiting for spring. Over tea and shortcake in the kitchen, he asked Eliza to marry him, but she turned him down. Although she admitted she would have liked to have had a home of her own and a baby or two to rock to sleep, she said no. She had to say no, didn't she? Hadn't she dedicated herself to Miss Braddie? There would be no changing horses.

Somehow the winter passed. On the third of March, Mr. and Mrs. Edward Spencer of Randallstown arrived at St. Michaels to spend a few days at Mount Pleasant. Looking back to the visit, Eliza said she could not remember a single thing—how everybody looked, what was said, what they had for dinner, nothing. To her dying day she'd remember only the glorious end of it. When Mr. and Mrs. Spencer left for Baltimore on *The Minnie Wheeler,* Eliza left with them.

Scared to death of the water, she stepped bravely aboard, carrying her possessions in two fat carpet bags. She went straight to the cabin, sat upright on a bench, full skirt hiding her shoes, and her bonnet strings tied in a tight knot under her determined chin.

When the engine began to throb and the side wheels began to turn, Miss Braddie came to the cabin door and said, "Are you all right, Liza?"

"Yes indeedy, Miss Braddie, yes indeedy. I am now."

"Liza, I'm glad you are with me again. I missed you very, very much."

Eliza ducked her head to hide her face. She didn't want anybody, not even Miss Braddie herself, to know the depth of her joy. Happy as she was, Eliza didn't dare to lean back. Not with all that water underneath and full of hungry sea monsters. Through the cabin porthole she watched Miss Braddie leaning on the rail pointing out a familiar landmark to her husband. This time tomorrow, the Lord willing, the Spencer family, all three of them—Miss Braddie, Marse Edward and Eliza—would be home at The Martin's Nest.

15

At The Martin's Nest

Eastern Bay was choppy that day. When *The Minnie Wheeler* rounded Bloody Point Light, Miss Braddie began to feel seasick. She retired to her stateroom and sent Edward to fetch Eliza. Setting aside fear of shipwreck, drowning, being swallowed by whales, and other dire calamities, Eliza hurried down the companionway.

She found Miss Braddie, face green and sweaty, lying on her bunk and lost no time comforting her with a damp towel laid across the forehead. As soon as Miss Braddie felt a little better, well enough to speak, she told Eliza she was not only plain old seasick, but she was also "in a family way."

Eliza was so pleased she covered her mouth with her hand to keep from chuckling out loud. A baby coming, Miss Braddie's own baby! Her lap was ready. Two to look after now, and soon there would be three. It was a blessed good thing Miss Em let loose when she did, a blessed good thing. For the first time Eliza appreciated all Miss Em had done for her, how she had trained her to be somebody. Some day maybe she could make it up to Miss Em for wilting on her, dying on the vine, being next to no good at all. She laid another cool towel across Miss Braddie's forehead. "It boun' to be de finess baby on earth, couldn't hep but be."

Presently there was a rap on the door and a man's voice said, "Mrs. Spencer, ma'am, kindly come to the saloon and fetch Mr. Spencer. He's gotten himself into a fight with a ruffian, and I fear for his life."

"I'll tend to it at once, thank you for telling me," Miss Braddie said, getting to her feet. She dropped back on the bunk again, sighing. "Oh dear, I can't make it, Liza. You go tend to it for me, please."

"Yes, Miss Braddie." How good it was to be on hand again. Eliza, picturing Marse Edward lying on the deck in a pool of blood, hurried aft to the saloon. The fight was over. Marse Edward was leaning against the bar breathing heavily, his chin-length hair flaring out like a chrysanthemum in full bloom, his cravat untied, his coat sleeve ripped at the shoulder. His cursing opponent was being forcefully escorted through the door by two sinister-looking cohorts. Nobody had to tell Eliza this was no time to speak or even be seen. She tiptoed away and returned to the stateroom.

"Marse Edward be all right soon's he cool down," she told Miss Braddie. "I hear de bartender tell a fellow de other man vex him beyond common endurance, braggin' 'bout de Union Army. He had to fight. Nothin' else he could do."

Miss Braddie said she supposed not, Edward being Edward. The rest of the trip was uneventful, as Eliza said, except for a three-hour layover in Annapolis harbor, where all incoming and outgoing boats were searched for runaway slaves. The rumor was that several were in the vicinity. Finally, *The Minnie Wheeler* went on to Baltimore where the tired travelers met with another delay. The lead horse of the Liberty Road Coach team had lost a shoe, and the blacksmith could not be found. He had been thrown in jail for speaking his mind, so it turned out.

Eventually the horse was shod by a blacksmith from another neighborhood, and the coach went on its way. Edward, up front with the driver, smoked his cigar and talked about the war, the fall of West Virginia at Rich Mountain and Corrick's Ford, and how Jackson rallied his men at Little Bull Run, held the hill and won the battle, winning for himself the name "Stonewall."

Inside the coach Miss Braddie and Eliza sat facing a tired woman, two small boys, a parrot, and a large bundle.

"Giddap there, Pete, Joe, giddap!" Whack! the whip cracked in the air, and the coach lurched on its way. In spite of deep ruts in the road that kept the coach rocking and swaying like a storm-tossed ship, Miss Braddie's calm, beautiful face did not turn green. For twelve miles she sat upright talking to the little boys, telling them about the sheep, pigs, horses, and chickens at the farm, listening to them tell about their parrot.

Eliza's bonnet slipped to one side, the false curls sewed in around the face dipping down over her eyes. Aside from that and the jolts, she was jubilant.

Home at last. "Whoa there, Pete, whoa boy." The coach stopped at the roadside, and the travelers stepped down. How good it felt to walk down the lane, pasture on one side, orchard on the other. Eliza, a step or so behind the other two, looked this way and that, sizing up The Martin's Nest. Although it couldn't hold a candle to Clay's Hope or Mount Pleasant, it had charm. The house on ahead made her think of a well-cut coat frayed at the cuffs. The lines were good, chimneys straight, roof not sagging much. Everything needed painting, though: house, barn, sheds, retainers, cabins, fences—everything.

"We're home, Mother," Marse Edward called out as he stepped on the porch. Right away Miss Spencer was there hugging Miss Braddie affectionately, then greeting her son, and Eliza, saying how glad she was to see them home again. She was all Marse Edward said she was in his letters: plump, warm, outgoing and pretty in a blue-eyed, fair-haired way. Eliza felt sure she was going to be easy to live with, not another Miss Em. Miss Em was all right—in fact she was much more than all right. Eliza missed her—nothing like the way she missed Miss Braddie those long lonely months of course, but she missed her. After all, she was Marse Bradford's own child, same as Miss Braddie was. No, not the same. Anyhow, she was Marse Bradford's, no getting around that.

Eliza went straight to the kitchen, which was inside the house at the back. She had never seen a kitchen inside before. It seemed strange, a new-fangled idea, she guessed. She inspected the cupboards, sniffed, opened the oven door, and measured it with an expert eye. The kitchen would do. She wasn't sure about Jane, the black girl who was cutting cabbage for slaw in a slipshod way as though she had all day and nothing else to do. After "Howdy," Eliza took off bonnet and shawl, put on an apron she found hanging behind the door, and said to Jane, "Han' me de knife an' lemme taste de dressin'." Jane obeyed. After tasting the dressing, Eliza smacked her lips and said with authority, "Need a speck more sugar, a dash a vinegar, an' three drops a sherry."

The way the girl followed directions it was easy to tell she was natural-born, fitted for second place. So far in her life, Eliza had always been in second place in the kitchen, but she was natural-born, fitted for first place, so fine and dandy.

When Eliza heard she was to share a room with Jane in the tenant house at the edge of the pasture, she balked and stuck out her lower lip and chin, way out. Miss Braddie knew that look. The storage room in the back of the dwelling house would do. It was small but private. Marse Edward moved trunks and boxes out and Eliza in. There was enough space for a cot and her belongings, but none to spare. Oh well, she wouldn't be there much anyway, busy as she would be from six in the morning until seven at night. How in the world Jane ever managed without her, Eliza didn't know.

Needed and appreciated—what could be better than that? Eliza said that one time during dinner Miss Spencer said, "This chicken pie is the best I ever tasted." Another time during breakfast Marse Edward praised the lace-edged flapjacks eloquently. She liked the way he had with words. Nobody spoke the way he did, nobody except maybe Marse Bradford when he was telling Tom how the apple orchard looked. Eliza part way remembered hearing him herself, as little as she was, and part way remembered from what Rosa and Mable said.

Eliza worried about Marse Edward. He worked too hard, farming daytime, writing at night. Even with The Dutchman to help, he worked too hard. Actually, the tenant farmer was German. It was Edward's mother who was Dutch. Eliza knew all that, but she called all foreigners Dutch People except those with questionable morals. They were French. Dutchman or no Dutchman, Marse Edward was wearing himself to the bone. At night Eliza could hear him pacing the floor in the study below her room, pacing and pacing till the stars faded. He had a lot on his mind as Miss Braddie filled out with the coming child: articles to write for the papers, and then there was the war. The war didn't seem real to Eliza, but it was as real as his own blood to Marse Edward.

By that time the Confederate Army was united under General Robert E. Lee. From what Marse Edward said about Marse Lee, Eliza knew what a fine gentleman he was. Surely the tide of war would go his way. For a while it did. The Union Army, beaten at the Second Battle of Bull Run, retreated to Washington, leaving behind a mound of dead Eliza couldn't imagine how high. Later on, Miss Braddie read in the newspaper that 1,481 northerners and almost as many southerners died in a few days, and over seven thousand were wounded on both sides. Eliza liked numbers. They were high sounding. She did not like to think of somebody crossing bloody fields counting dead and dying men. Numbers should be pure numbers, not stand for people dead or alive.

One day the realness of war reached her ears. She would never forget it. She was hanging clothes on the line out behind the house when she heard thunder. Thunder with the sky robin-egg blue and not a cloud?

"Miss Braddie, come listen!" she called out in fear. Miss Braddie, Marse Edward, Miss Spencer and even

Jane came running. "Gunfire," Edward said, his face twisted with anguish. "The wind must be blowing directly this way from Antietam, fifty miles away."

BOOM, BOOM, BRRROOM! Faint as the sound was, it was chilling.

BOOM, BOOM BRROOOM!

Miss Braddie took Marse Edward's hand, and he said, "It's Lee and Jackson facing McClellan. They've been lined up near Sharpsburg for days, waiting. God how I wish I were there to fight with them!"

More numbers—75,000 Union soldiers and 51,000 Confederates lost. And the wounded were so many it was a wonder their cries didn't travel fifty miles on the wind. The following year, sounds of the Battle of Gettysburg reached The Martin's Nest, but between the two battles the home news pushed war news into second place. Miss Braddie's baby was born, Edward Spencer III.

"Don't cry ... Mammy's here," Eliza said, holding the baby in her arms for the first time. He fit her shoulder as though it had been fashioned especially for him. She was so proud, so overjoyed. Miss Braddie and Marse Edward were proud, too, and so was Miss Spencer, proud and happy in spite of the war.

Happiness soon turned to sorrow. Nobody knew why the baby died, but he did. Perfectly formed, marble white and still, the imprint of him never left Eliza. Never. During the next two years, another baby was born to Miss Braddie and Marse Edward, and it died. Eliza said those little graves were enough to tear your heart out. Two dead were ten times more than ten thousand to Eliza. Yes, there she was Mammy and no baby. Sad, so sad.

At The Martin's Nest

While General U. S. Grant and the Union Army "burst upon Virginia" and marched down the Shenandoah Valley between General Lee and Richmond, while casualties piled up at The Wilderness, Spotsylvania Court House (those "eleven days in May" of heavy fighting that included the death of Lee's beloved Jeb Stuart at Yellow Tavern), and while Major General Sherman's march wound its way through the south with cities, countryside, and men falling before him—all that time Eliza comforted Miss Braddie. She did the only thing she could, saying nothing. She worked with her day by day.

Poor Marse Edward worked the best way he could, feeling the loss of his babies, feeling the war turning against the South, feeling angry that his eyes kept him out of the army. Miss Braddie's sorrow was deeper perhaps than his. Eliza thought that Miss Spencer and Miss Braddie were as brave as any soldiers. They lived out each day, and when the upswing came, they were ready for it.

The start of the upswing, not in the war but at home, was the birth of Robert Leigh Spencer in 1864. He was a scrawny, bug-eyed baby, not a bit pretty, but he lived.

Alleluia! He lived and kept on living.

Eliza was truly Mammy now. Rocking the cradle with her foot, she knitted and sang her own version of a hymn Rosa used to sing back at Clay's Hope in the days before the war:

> "Put John on the Island when the
> bridegroom comes
> Put John on the Island when he
> comes

A Promise is to Keep

O, put John on the Island, put
    John on the Island
Put John on the Island when he
    comes.
The ravens came and fed him
    over there
The ravens came and fed him
    over there
O, the ravens came and fed him
The ravens came and fed him
The ravens came and fed him
    over there."

When Rob was two, Lindsly was born. When Lindsly was three, Emily was born. Three years later, along came Beverley Brown and last of all, Katharine Constable.

"Beverley Brown died when he was a dear little boy not five years old," Eliza told me. "Yes, died he did and was buried in a graveyard with two dead babies."

Seeing my full-of-sorrow face, she added, "No use you frettin', honey. Joy lost no time taking the reins. The other four children lived and kept on livin'."

"Put John on the Island when the bridegroom comes!"

Alleluia!

16

People and Politics

Years later when Eliza was old and I was young, we were in the kitchen at Nancy's Fancy. She was peeling apples for a pie, and I was watching. What an expert she was, one long unbroken apple peel dangling down from the paring knife like a red Christmas tree ornament.

"Eliza," I said, chin in my hands, elbows on the table. "Tell me about my grandfather Edward Spencer. I know what he did and all; even so, I don't know him as a person, what he was like. He wrote all those letters and a lot besides when he wasn't suffering from sorrow and stewing about politics and the war."

Eliza's face crinkled with amusement. Selecting another apple from the slat basket beside the table, she said, "Ever notice how when your father grind his axe sparks fly?"

I nodded. "That's what Marse Edward like. Sparks fly off him right and lef'. Miss Braddie know what she doin' when she married him. Time an' again servin' dinner I hear him fling a idea to her across de' table an' she polish it off an' fling it back. An' laugh—you shoulda heard those two laugh together. Sometime I'd haf to hurry outa de room to keep from joinin' in. Miss Em tell me never to join in, and she know what's proper an' what isn't. Ol' Miss Spencer join in. Oft times she de butt a de merriment. Like de time she got herself stuck on top a de pasture fence. 'Ed-ward! Edward!' I hear her call. 'Come hep me down 'fore de buzzards spy me!' Right away he come runnin' an' laughin'. He pull an' lift an' grunt 'til down she fall on top a him. Like to squash him flat, portly as she was. Together dey laugh fit to bust dere side. De Spencers all great laughers. Up an' down dey manage to fine somepin' to tickle dere ribs."

Satisfied that I knew my grandfather a little bit better, I said, "Now tell me about the children, Eliza. I don't mean us, Ruth, Catherine, and me. I mean the Spencer children: Mother and her sister and brothers. Tell me about them when they were children."

Eliza went on paring. After a while she said, "When your Uncle Robbie, Master Rob, Miss Braddie's oldest chile was one year old, de war ended."

"The Civil War?" I asked, polishing an apple on my sleeve.

"What else? After Master Rob born an' befo' Master Lindsly come along, de fightin' stop an' Marse Robert E. Lee had to han' over his sword to I forget who an' where."

"To General Ulysses S. Grant at Appomattox Court House on April 9, 1865," I told her in my best schoolbook language.

"Dat it," Eliza said. "A whole lot a livin' cram into dose years. Poor President Lincoln got hisself killed. Now I didn't cotton to him de way some did. Even so, a man got a right to go to de theatre an' come back home again to sleep in his own bed."

114

I agreed to that. "Yes, the assassination of Abraham Lincoln was the most dreadful thing that ever happened. Fortunately, though, his Emancipation Proclamation was tended to before he died. You should be glad of that, Eliza, being a slave yourself."

"Me be glad he turn loose all my people, turn dem outa house an' home, trained an' untrained, young an' old, to root hog or die? Where dey go? Dey got to eat an' who gonna feed 'em? Dey got to work an' who pay 'em for doin' what? Least he could do be ship 'em back to where dey come from so's dey could make a fresh start. No, he had to turn 'em loose, widout even a mule to ride on."

"I don't know, but I do know for sure that slavery is wrong and freedom is right. People must be paid for work they do. How much did my grandfather pay you, Eliza, after you were free?"

"What you mean pay me?" Eliza said with indignation. "Marse Edward know better than to insult me wid money. We all work together, him, Miss Braddie, Miss Spencer, an' me. We a fam'ly. Freedom got nothin' to do wid fam'ly, nor money neither." She thought a moment before adding, "Now Viney free, do fine fer herself, I speck. When a field han' gone off de lan', who do de plantin' an' pickin'? Nobody got money to pay anybody. Money in de land itself an' in de seed."

"Machine reapers and that sort of thing do the work now," I told her.

Eliza fetched nutmeg and brown sugar and butter for the pie and then peeled one last apple. "After de war Marse Edward make some money wid his writin' again. He make enough fer us all to eat an' keep de roof from leakin'. Mebbe he'd had some to put in bank if didn't have his brother's fam'ly to feed an' look after besides his own. Master Bob, he come outa de war alive, thin as a rail, poor as Job's turkey, nervous an' high strung as a wild cat. All he own was clothes on his back an' a wife an' two daughters used to easy street. He lay down his gun an' went out West saying he'd send fer his fam'ly once he settle somewheres."

As I knew more was coming, I didn't say anything, just waited. Eliza crisscrossed the pie with crust strips. "Soon's he outa sight his wife, your Aunt Emma, she hitch up de mare, swing de girls an' luggage into de carriage an' out de road she drive to de Martin's Nest to pay us a visit. There six weeks, she up an' had herself a baby, a boy name a Meredith. Can't feed two, so she had three. An' de followin' spring de mare had a colt.

"Three years. I didn't mind her takin' de baby when she lef'. Still it seem to me she shoulda lef' de colt. Those days were hard an' good. Hard work an' good, Miss Braddie, Miss Spencer, an' me keepin' house side by side, de chillen growing up 'round us. I kin see dem all: Master Rob, tall an' slim as a willow stick; Master Coos—we called Master Lindsly 'Coos'—short like his father an' funny. There never was a funnier chile on dis earth dan Master Coos. An' den dere was your mother, Miss Em'ly."

Eliza sat down in the chair by the table and repeated "Miss Em'ly" as though the name had a whole lot rolled into it. "She the closest thing to bein' Miss Braddie on dis earth. Not in looks 'cept fer black eyes an' straight black hair. She like her in spirit. Miss Em'ly would give you anythin' she had if she thought you wanted it. Last of all was de baby, Katharine, your Aunt Tat. I kin still feel her sittin' on my lap."

116

"What about us, my sisters and me?" I asked frowning. "Don't you feel us sitting on your lap?"

"Yes indeedy," Eliza answered. "Plain as day fer a fact I do. Miss Ruth weigh a ton, Miss Catherine pretty as a han' paintin' an' you, Miss Nan, sittin' bolt upright, not leanin' back."

I narrowed my eyes and looked at Eliza through the slits. Although she was old, wrinkled, and worn-out, her spirit was frisky as a young squirrel's. I closed my eyes and willed her back to The Martin's Nest, back to when my mother was a little girl and I wasn't anywhere at all.

17

Shiny Bright Needle

It had snowed all night and most of the morning. The Martin's Nest sparkled, flaws hidden under magic white. House, barn, sheds were frosted like wedding cakes. The trees wore lace, and fields slept under new blankets. Marse Edward and the boys, Rob and Coos, had gone to Randallstown in the sleigh to fetch the mail, bells jingling, horse stepping high.

In the house Miss Braddie sat at the desk in the front room writing a letter to Miss Em. Over in front of the open fire, old Miss Spencer was toasting her toes and reading her son's newest play.

Back in the kitchen, Jane snoozed near the stove, head lolling to one side, mouth open, arms limp on her lap, the Mother Cat asleep under her chair. Eliza was sewing by the window; six-year-old Emily and two-year-old Katharine leaned against her knees watching her shiny bright needle. Eliza was making a yellow calico dress for Emily's doll. Katharine preferred her doll to be undressed. Hugs had turned its white rolled-sheet body to gray. Kisses had smudged its features.

Both girls looked up into Eliza's face at the same

moment, their eyes full of expectation. She knew what they wanted. The old songs and games Rosa, Mable, and Tom used to sing and play in the days of Clay's Hope, that's what.

She tapped her foot, hidden by full skirt and many petticoats. When she was satisfied that the meter was right, she sang.

> "Lost my needle
> Yes ma'am
> Shiny bright needle
> Yes ma'am
> Hep me to find it
> Yes ma'am."

"More!" Katharine demanded and Emily said, "Black Sheep next."

Eliza, a natural-born entertainer, stuck her needle into the narrow collar of her shirtwaist for safekeeping. Then lifting her hands, she wiggled her fingers, getting them ready to act out their parts.

> "Eliza and Daddy and Uncle John
> Went to market on a black sheep
> Eliza fell off
> Daddy fell off
> And away went Uncle John."

The girls clapped their hands and shouted, "More, more" as Katharine's doll dropped to the floor with a thud. The little girl stooped to pick it up, hugged it to her, and waited with her big sister for act three.

Eliza thought a moment before reciting her father's favorite.

A Promise is to Keep

"Possum up de gum tree
Raccoon in de holler
Wake Jake
June bug
Stole a half a dollar."

Emily recited it after her. Then, pulling on Eliza's sleeve, she said, "Come on, let's play In and Out the Windows. Want to?"

Eliza declared she wanted to well enough, but they needed the boys to help out: three was too few to play. Seeing Emily's crestfallen face she said, "Mus' be somepin' else we could do."

"Yes. Tyson's Bull," Emily said, her eyes dancing. "And after that The Buzzards."

Laying her sewing aside, Eliza stood up. Standing in the middle of the kitchen floor, she faced the audience frowning, her cheeks puffed out to bull proportions. She pawed the ground with her feet, pretending to send dirt flying out behind as she "bellered" ferociously. "I want to know de *reason* why I can't get any *rye* straw."

The girls shivered with terror so Eliza bellered again for good measure. The air was still charged with anticipation, but Eliza said, "Dat's all," and sat down and picked up her sewing.

"You forgot The Buzzards," Emily told her.

"So I did."

She sewed awhile, just long enough to whip her audience up into a state of bursting. "One day a aggregation a buzzards were sailin' 'round de sky, wings spread wide not flappin', jes' sailin' easy like."

After a long pause, Eliza went on. "By an' by ol' Boss

Shiny Bright Needle

Buzzard, he spy a dead hog at de edge a de woods. He drop straight down like a stone an' landed near de dead hog. One by one de res' a de aggregation follow suit 'til de whole gee-navy of 'em had joined him."

Emily, who knew the story by heart, leaned heavily on Eliza's lap, and Katharine did too. This was the good part.

"The buzzards, dey circle 'round de hog, circle 'round him, circle 'round him. After while ol' Boss Buzzard, he stop close to hog's head an' he say deep down in his throat:

'Be-gin
Be-gin'

On a high note the other buzzards say,

'Where 'bouts
Where 'bouts?'

Old Boss Buzzard answer deep:

'In his eye, in his eye
Pluck it out, pluck it out.'

"An' right away dey all pitch in an' pick de bones a dat hog clean." Hand to her ear, Eliza said, "Listen . . . sleigh bells!"

With shouts of "Papa's comin'," the girls ran to the window. Jane woke up, rocked on the cat's tail, and sent the poor creature streaking into the front room.

"No sign a de sleigh yet," declared Eliza, her nose pressed flat against the window pane. "All I see is Crazy Ritter."

"Oooo !" the girls cried, dashing for the safety of the cupboard. They knew Crazy Ritter was a harmless man who wandered around the neighborhood; even so, his name was a bug-a-boo that scared them.

"Here dey come," Eliza said. "Here come de sleigh."

A Promise is to Keep

Emily and Katharine fell out of the cupboard along with three tin lids and the preserving kettle. "Father and the boys are home," they reported in loud voices as they ran down the hall spreading the news. And back they came to Eliza without slowing up.

The merry sound of sleigh bells stopped down by the barn. Presently Marse Edward came in the back door, stamped his feet on the mat to knock off the snow, and with a "Good day, Eliza" and a greeting to his daughters, he joined his wife and mother in the living room. Two minutes later, pandemonium: Rob and Coos burst in, red-cheeked, snow flying in all directions.

"I'm hungry, Eliza," Coos said, tossing his cap at the wall peg by the window and missing. He flopped on the floor, holding both feet in the air. "Emily, my boots."

Emily struggled to pull off Rob's boots. "I'll be with you shortly, Coos, soon's I finish here," said Emily, whereupon Eliza declared the boys should be ashamed of themselves, big as they were, for making their little sister wait on them.

"We don't make her do anything," Rob said. "She likes to wait on us hand and foot. She'd go through fire and water for us. You would, wouldn't you, Emily?"

Emily giggled happily and Eliza knew why. She herself would go through fire and water for any one of the children. Turning to Jane, she said, "How come you standin' dere doin' nothin' an' de chillen hungry? Lif' down de cookie jar an' set out de cups whilst I make cocoa."

"Lunch only half hour off," Jane said with a yawn, her eye on the kitchen clock.

"What dat got to do wid it?" Eliza said. "Dey hungry now."

Shiny Bright Needle

Five minutes later the four children were around the table sipping hot cocoa and munching cookies. Eliza stood back by the stove and looked at them, Miss Braddie's own flesh and blood. Each one was special: Rob, the oldest, was mighty close. Hadn't she rocked him to sleep a year and more before Coos was born? Snap-and-jerking Coos, the image of his father, always into something, always full of fun. And Miss Em'ly, sitting there licking her finger tip, was pure gold through and through. Big-eyed Katharine was the baby, Miss Braddie's and Eliza's baby.

It was a good thing Eliza felt the way she did about the Spencer children, for the time was coming when they would have her and little else.

18

Heart Break

Before the snow melted, Emily played a joke on the family, Emily, not Coos. She slipped out the kitchen door when Eliza wasn't looking, ran down to the barn, and climbed up in the sleigh. With both hands, she shook the sleigh bells in trot time so expertly that everybody thought company was coming up the lane. Faces appeared at windows—Marse Edward's and his mother's upstairs, Eliza's, Miss Braddie's, and Jane's downstairs. Rob and Coos poked heads out the front door. The horses looked over the fence.

Emily ran back to the house laughing, leaping high in the air shouting, "April fool!" January notwithstanding. The day was referred to thereafter as the day Emily April-fooled everybody. She tried it again, but nobody was fooled except the horses and Jane.

Two more snows and winter was over; spring came again. Birds built nests in the trees, delicate green came to life in all directions, and hearts were light. Then came gloom. The Spencers were moving to town.

"Not a bit a use you standin' dere lookin' like Granny Doodie's chile, Miss Em'ly," Eliza said as she wrapped one of the best cups in newspaper to pack in the barrel. "We movin' cause we must, an' when you must do somethin' you do it. Your father too far from what's goin' on fer too long a time a'ready. From way out here in de country, time his editorials get to town dey too stale to print. It take more dan a play or two an' a batch a poems to send de boys to Princeton an' de girls to wherever Miss Braddie say. Besides dat, Marse Edward got a gift a friendship an' it dryin' up out here."

Miss Em'ly kept on looking hang-dog, so Eliza gave her a job to do. "Here, wrap de saucers an' mind you don't drop 'em." Coos, who was standing in the doorway, spoke up, "What about de horses, de pigs, de cows an' all?"

Before Eliza had a chance to reply, Rob came in and complained in a peeved tone of voice, "Yeah, and what about Grandmother and Jane?" Eliza answered, "Miss Spencer go wid us, a course. Jane an' de animals stay here to live wid de people who gonna live here after we gone."

Right then Katharine came in with the Mother Cat in her arms. "Put her down," ordered Emily fiercely. "You're squeezing her guts."

"Don't say guts, honey," Eliza said. "Say entrails. It soun' better."

Emily snatched the cat from her sister, further imperiling the entrails, and said, "She goes with us or I'm not going."

To everybody's joy, Eliza said, "She kin go ef she live 'til movin' day. Master Rob, you an' Master Coos roll dis full barrel over in de corner an' roll de empty one over here. We got a mess a work to do."

The Mother Cat survived and moved to 294 Stricker

A Promise is to Keep

Street, Baltimore, Maryland, with the Spencer family. Marse Edward and Miss Braddie and Miss Spencer went on ahead in the carriage to be there when the furniture arrived. Eliza and the children traveled to town on the Liberty Road coach, looking like immigrants. Rob carried the grandmother clock, which kept ticking fast, the pendulum weight in his pocket for safekeeping. Coos carried a bird nest and a bucketful of stones he had collected over the years and couldn't live without. Emily held her doll in one arm and lugged the doll trunk in the other hand. Katharine needed both arms for her doll.

"More on your back, less in hand," Eliza said. To prove it, she had on two skirts over three petticoats, two shirtwaists, a cape, and the bonnet with curls attached over her head handkerchief. She carried the Mother Cat, who required both hands and constant vigilance.

Spirits of cat and children were low. "No wonder everybody wild-eyed an' long-faced," Eliza said. "Uprooted from the onlies' home you ever knew, a body boun' to pine." Riding along toward town, horses trotting, coach swaying and jolting, she did her best to cheer them up, saying things would be fine once they got where they were going. "You'll see," she said cheerfully.

They saw, all right, that 294 Stricker Street, described to me years later by Eliza, was narrow as a chicken house, the backyard not much bigger than Marse Edward's pool table. It had no front yard at all and no porch. Five white marble steps led from brick sidewalk to door. The hall was narrow and dark.

"Welcome home, everybody!" Miss Braddie called

from upstairs. Spirits lifted. The cat sprang out of Eliza's arms, scooted up the steps and hid, nobody knew where. Eliza took off her bonnet, tied on her apron, and the work of settling in began. There were curtains to hang, rugs to unroll, beds to make, and lunch to get. What a job! She had never been busier.

In spite of missing the farm, everybody except Coos and the Mother Cat were soon reasonably happy in the new house. Those two were reasonably unhappy. The cat came out of hiding only when driven by hunger. Coos fumed about, pacing up and down like a caged lion, tripping over rockers and his own feet, complaining loudly. "I can't breathe around here. There isn't enough air. There isn't enough space. I hate it in town!"

Even Eliza failed to console him. Then one day he discovered the street and all complaining stopped. It didn't take him any time to round up a gang of boys his age and it didn't take the gang any time to discover Eliza and her handouts—bread-and-butter-and-sugar, ginger cookies, and on rare occasions, fried chicken wings to eat in your hand.

There was a new school for the children, a new church for everybody, a new market, a new butcher at the door, peddlers selling needles and pins.

"Fresh fish, buy your fresh fish!"

"Fruit, Missus, picked this morning, apples, pears, tomatoes!"

Eliza was busy and humming happily. Best of all was serving tea in the front room to ladies from church: Miss Braddie, pretty as a picture, her back straight as a poker, her black hair shining, and pouring tea; over by the window Miss Spencer, plumper than ever, dressed in her best silk dress, talking with the rector's wife.

A Promise is to Keep

Marse Edward's company came in the evening and stayed late, smoking cigars, sipping brandy, and talking. Politics, Eliza guessed, and from the bursts of laughter she knew the conversation was generously sprinkled with wit. Marse Edward was where he belonged. Because he was, it was right to give up horses, garden at the back door, orchards in bloom, birds singing at the first sign of dawn, and the children swinging high in the rope swing on the strong limb of the walnut tree by the spring. Yes, town was best for Marse Edward. What was best for him was best for Miss Braddie, and what was best for Miss Braddie was best for Eliza.

The feeling in the air was that Marse Edward was doing fairly well, though not well enough to suit him. To help pay bills that continued to arrive with alarming regularity, he decided to take a job of some sort, not necessarily tied to his writing: He failed to secure a professorship at St. John's College in Annapolis; he failed to win a political appointment in the Baltimore Customs House; he failed to be appointed librarian at the Peabody Institute.

Bitterly hating failure of any kind, he wrote with renewed vigor and determination.

After a change in management of *The World,* he was on the staff of *The Bulletin,* and he worked at night with Thomas Scharf on *The History of Maryland.* Later on he worked with William Hand Brown on the *Life of Bayard Taylor.* Still later he became an editorial writer for *The Baltimore Sun.* Eliza did not know the details of all his goings on. Never mind, it was enough to know that the older children were at school. Miss Katharine stayed home waiting to be old enough to go to school. Miss Braddie and Miss Spencer were busy doing their part keeping house.

Then came a change, a dismal change. The cat died and was buried under the rose bush in the backyard. "Grieved herself to death," Eliza declared. "Pining for de mice in de barn an' for her ol' huntin' ground she grieved herself away." With solemnity she was buried, her grave dug by Coos. With Miss Braddie, Eliza, and Katharine standing by, Rob read the burial service. Emily watched from the upstairs back window with round, serious eyes. After the ceremony, Eliza told her the Mother Cat was in heaven, and Emily replied, "She'll hate it there. She likes it where we are."

That was Emily's first encounter with death. It was not her last. The following year Miss Spencer died of pneumonia and was buried in the cemetery alongside Miss Braddie's dead babies.

The day of Miss Spencer's funeral was the worst: cold, rainy, windy. There never was a day to match it. Eliza said she tried her best to make Miss Braddie stay home saying, "You catch graveyard pneumonia yourself, standin' on soggy ground."

Miss Braddie would go, and Eliza stayed home with the girls. Miss Braddie stood on the soggy ground beside her husband and sons until the last Amen. As Eliza predicted, she caught cold, a heavy cold that settled in her chest. The cold hung on, and Eliza worried. She was glad when Marse Edward called in the doctor and gladder still when the doctor said Miss Braddie did not have pneumonia, that she'd be fine when summer came.

But Miss Braddie was not fine when summer came. She coughed and kept on coughing. Every night at bed time Eliza rubbed her chest with camphorated oil, and every day she took upon her own shoulders a little bit more of Miss Braddie's work.

"You res' yourself, honey," she'd say again and again. "Res' an' let Liza look after de house an' de chillen."

Eliza worked in silence. There would be no singing or humming until the coughing stopped. As time went on, Marse Edward could not work. Haunted by the memory of the death of his beloved brother Tom and his mother, he sat at his desk staring at the blank sheet of paper before him, unable to write a word.

Every night when the children were in bed, the dishes washed, and the house ready for tomorrow, Eliza knelt beside her bed and prayed to the Good Lord for Miss Braddie and for Marse Edward who loved her so. She also prayed for herself for strength to face the dreadful truth that had to be faced. Miss Braddie had consumption.

Slowly, painfully, racked by coughing, and her cheeks flushed, Miss Braddie went downhill. On February 12, 1882, her forty-first birthday, she was too weak to come downstairs to her own birthday party. The family gathered around her bed. Rob gave her a wooden tray he'd made in the cellar. Coos gave her his prized chestnut whistle, made at the farm and in his pocket all the time. Katharine gave her red beads she had strung herself. Emily gave her a water color of The Martin's Nest painted from memory. Marse Edward's gift was a new poem, and Eliza's was a birthday cake, three tiers, with white icing—the kind Miss Braddie liked best.

Two weeks later, February 27, Miss Braddie died. Eliza, standing beside the bed, saw the black eyes close for the last time and felt her own heart break. She must not give in to grief, not now. Not with her own work to do and Miss Braddie's. She had the children to look after and Marse Edward. She must not give in to her own sorrow. Twelve-year-old Miss Em'ly, defenseless and wide-open to suffering, wouldn't let go of her skirt. Eliza couldn't think about herself now.

Poor Marse Edward. He wanted to help but couldn't. Years later when Eliza told me about Miss Braddie's death she said, "It was a good thing de minister at Ascension Church saw to it Miss Braddie was buried in de fam'ly lot, a blessed good thing, for nobody else could think, only feel." Then she told me about what happened after the funeral.

The next day she sent the children off to school as usual: shoes shined, hair brushed, lunches packed. When they came home, she was at the door to greet them. At supper time, she set before them a good hot meal. She wished Marse Edward would come downstairs to dine with his children. She called him again and again and so did Rob, but he didn't come down. He couldn't, she reckoned.

For weeks he stayed in his room, the door shutting him in and the rest of the family out. Eliza said she took his meals up to him on a tray, knowing Miss Braddie would want her to. The friends who stopped by to see him he sent away.

Edward Spencer lived one year and four months after Miss Braddie died. Plagued by grief, insomnia, nervous prostration, and a return of a kidney ailment that had bothered him for years, he died at his doctor's office on Fayette Street. He left behind no money, some debts, a drawer full of manuscripts, four children, and Eliza—and a poem.

Eliza said she was on hand out in the hall the day Miss Braddie sat down at her piano for the last time.

A Promise is to Keep

She heard her play and sing for her husband, standing close-by, the songs they knew together.

"It was twelve-year-old Miss Em'ly who read de poem aloud dat day—aloud to her brother, her sister, an' me," Eliza said. Years later, I found a copy of the poem, a clipping from *The Baltimore Sun,* in Miss Emily's scrapbook. It was called "Remembered Music" by Edward Spencer.

> Before her mind went out to sea
> My little wife she said to me:
> "Come down, dear man, and hear
>   me touch
> The chords you valued once so
>   much:
> The dust that gathers on the keys
> Will suit my old-time melodies."
> Thus said my little wife to me
> Before her mind went out to sea.
>
> Before her mind went out to sea
> She'd put on gay attire for me;
> Her hands, inspired by some soft
>   spell,
> Gently upon the keyboard fell.
> And oh, the chords the touch
>   awoke,
> What far, far whispers in them
>   spoke,
> As played my little wife for me
> Before her mind went out to sea!
>
> Before her mind went out to sea

Heart Break

My little wife turned round to
    me:
"I think you know this tune," she
    said—
She played it first when we were
    wed—
"And this?" I'd known it ere her
    hand—
So slender now—an octave
    spanned.
Oh, Christ, those pangs of melody
Before her mind went out to sea!

Before her mind went out to sea
My little wife thus played to me:
A pallid touch, remote, subdued,
But flushed to me with maiden-
    hood;
A simple song, a far-off chime,
A broken chord, a dropping
    rhyme—
And so our lifetime's symphony
Said out my little wife to me.

Before her mind went out to sea
Thus dreamed my little wife to
    me,
And as she played I dreamed
    again,
Of school-day loiterings in the
    lane:
Of love that peeped and love that
    sighed

A Promise is to Keep

Of love that would not be de-
    nied.
Oh, love! how played my wife for
    me
Before her mind went out to sea!

Before her mind went out to sea
She fondled thus with memory,
But always pleasant, as she oft
Returned with iteration soft,
Avoiding still the sterner rhymes
That hint of darkened, somber
    times:
For she was pitiful to me
Before her mind went out to sea.

Before her mind went out to sea
My little wife she played to me,
And never drew one single sigh
But always love-looks in her
    eye—
Oh, God! the sob that rent my
    breast!
"Dear Love," she whispered, "let
    us rest"—
Her lips to mine she pressed for
    me,
And then her mind went out to
    sea!

19

Eliza Makes a Speech

After Marse Edward's funeral when the last guest had left the house, the Spencer children sat in the kitchen with Eliza. Emily had the hiccups from crying, and Katharine held in her fist a wet ball of a handkerchief. There didn't seem to be anything to do or say. Everybody just sat listening to the clock tick time away. Finally, newspaper in hand, Rob said, "*The Baltimore Sun,* Wednesday morning, July 18, 1883. I'm going to read what it says about father." As he read aloud, Eliza kept nodding, "Dat's so, dat's so." When he came to the end of the eulogy, she said, "It lef' out how gentle an' kind he was, an' how much fun he an' Miss Braddie had together. An' how he took care a his mother to her dyin' day, an' how he looked after his brother's fam'ly. I speck we de only ones know him through an' through."

The children agreed, and Coos said he liked best what the *New York World* said about his father. "What was it, Rob? I forget the exact words."

Rob didn't remember, but Emily did. Hiccupping only once, she quoted proudly, "Edward Spencer was one of the most gifted men of the South, a man of encyclopedic information and powerful imagination." Then she burst into fresh tears and ran into the dining room.

"Set de table for supper, Miss Em'ly," Eliza called after her, and when Coos suggested that they eat in the kitchen, she said, "No indeedy, Miss Braddie wouldn't cotton to dat at all. From now on Marse Rob will sit at de head of de dinin' room table in Marse Edward's place. Miss Em'ly will sit in Miss Braddie's chair at de foot of de dinin' room table."

From now on. Those were sobering words to Eliza. If they were living on the farm she might be able to manage with plenty of eggs, milk, fresh vegetables and fruit in season, and with enough to can for winter. She could let down dresses for the girls as they grew tall and she could make shirts and pants for the boys out of clothes their father left behind. She couldn't make shoes, though, and already Rob's big toes were complaining.

Maybe somebody in the family would help. Not Miss Emily Harrison. Cousin Willie was dead, and she was living with her married daughter the best way she could. Cousin Willie drowned right at his own dock, which Eliza said she found hard to believe for he was as much at home in the water as out. Still, drown he did.

Miss Braddie's sister Mary, the one who lived in Philadelphia, had all she could do to take care of her own family. Miss Braddie's brothers would be no help either: Marse Jonathan was in Texas, most of his land gone, and all of his money spent in the war; The older one, Marse Sam the doctor, was sixty years old and in poor health himself, so she had heard.

As for the Spencer side of the family, no one was left

except Marse Edward's brother Bob, and nobody knew where he was or if he were still living.

"Somethin' bound to turn up soon," Eliza told the children, and she was right. Something did turn up. A notice came from the court house requesting the children of The Late Edward Spencer to appear in court the following Thursday at ten o'clock in the morning.

At quarter to ten, the four Spencers were sitting in a row on the long bench in the hall outside the judge's chambers, five counting Eliza. According to her, Rob, wearing too-tight, too-short pants, too-small coat, and his Sunday too-short shoes, sat on the end. Next to him sat Coos in Rob's hand-me-downs, his hair plastered flat as a fried flounder. Emily, next to Coos, wore a dress made out of Miss Braddie's green and blue striped skirt. Her hair was tied back with a black velvet ribbon, and she carried a large black velvet bag in which was a lavender handkerchief and the silver medal she won in elocution. Katharine, sitting between her sister and Eliza, had on a most becoming new red calico. Both girls wore bonnets.

Eliza said she had on a bonnet too, the one she always wore with curls attached. Under it and completely hidden, she wore the white head handkerchief. She never appeared without that, so she said, not even to cook breakfast. Although the day was warm, she had on a plaid shawl for style.

At ten-fifteen by the hall clock, the Spencers were ushered into the judge's chambers. Several men were already there talking together in the back of the room. One, a young man with a droopy mustache, appeared to be the court secretary. The others were dignified older men dressed in frock coats and cravats. The judge himself had a strong, kind face, which Eliza found reassuring.

The reassurance did not last, however, for the first time he opened his mouth, he referred to the children as "unfortunate orphans." Eliza bristled with indignation. Nobody, judge or anybody else, had a right to call Miss Braddie's children unfortunate orphans. Until that moment, Eliza had been afraid of thousand legs, bats, thunder and lightning, fast horses, and nothing else. She was afraid of nothing else until now.

Nevertheless, Eliza summoned her courage and stood up to speak her mind. She had to. Before she had a chance to say one word, the young man with the droopy mustache told her to sit down.

She sat, her jaw jutting out like the bow of a ship.

The judge cleared his throat and continued using the word orphans twice more in one sentence. Eliza told me she got to her feet a second time and before anyone could stop her said, "The chillen are not orphans, Your Honor. Dey have me. I stan' in Miss Braddie's stead now she an' Marse Edward both gone."

The judge nodded and smiled, saying something about dedication and loyalty. Then to Eliza's dismay he suggested that a foster home for each of the children would be the best solution to the problem, adding in a benevolent tone, "The court will do all in its power to place the two girls in the same home."

Eliza, still on her feet, said firmly: "Dere will be no separatin' de fam'ly. Miss Braddie wouldn't put up wid it nor Marse Edward neither. De four chillen mus' be together." She told me that right then Katharine hopped up and flung her arms around Eliza's knees and wailed. "I hate him! I hate him, Eliza! Make him go away and leave us alone!" Whereupon Rob leaned forward saying, "Emily, make her sit down and keep quiet."

As Emily pulled her little sister down beside her, the judge looked directly at Eliza: "Eliza . . . that is your name, is it not?"

"Born Eliza Ann Benson, Eliza Ann Spencer from now on," Eliza replied.

The judge continued. "Eliza, I appreciate your concern for the Spencer children and understand your desire to keep them together. Therefore, I shall commit them to the state orphanage where they will be well cared for together."

"Orphanage!" Eliza said. She had never felt as furious in her life. "Miss Braddie's chillen in a orphanage! Not as long as dere is breath in my body."

"Perhaps you can find a room nearby so as to visit them from time to time," the judge suggested, touching his fingertips together.

Eliza was still angry. "No, Your Honor. From time to time won't do. I got to be on han' all de time. How else kin I bring dem up de way Miss Braddie want? I know e-zackly how she an' Marse Edward want dem reared an' I am de onlies' one on earth do know. For me to go out to work, hire myself out, wouldn't do yet awhile. Miss Braddie wouldn't want de chillen comin' home from school to an empty house. Wid de Lord's help, I kin manage somehow."

Her heart pounding, Eliza sat down and folded her hands in her lap, so she told me. After a long silence, the heavyset gentleman in the back of the room, the one with the toothbrush mustache and full goatee, stood and asked for permission to speak.

"Granted, Mr. McCoy," the judge said, nodding his head with approval. "The court has long been cognizant of your newspaper work and your philanthropic endeavors in behalf of our city. Speak, by all means." Eliza remembered those big words—carried them in the back of her head all those years.

Mr. McCoy thanked the judge and then said, "I am deeply moved by Eliza, Your Honor, by her sure faith and her devotion to Mr. and Mrs. Spencer and their children. I believe, as she does, that no one else could bring them up as well as she could. Therefore, with the court's permission, I shall send to her regularly fifty dollars a month to be used as she thinks best for as long as she deems necessary."

Those present gave him a standing ovation, even the judge stood and clapped. Not Eliza. Overcome with emotion, she bent her head, struggling to keep back tears of joy. As soon as the clapping died down, the judge said how pleased he was at the outcome of the hearing, how generous Mr. McCoy was, how fortunate the children were to have him as their benefactor, and how fortunate they were to have Eliza to care for them. After assuming aloud that the proceeds from the sale of 294 Stricker Street and Mr. Spencer's valuable library would be sufficient to pay all debts against the estate, he declared that the hearing was over.

Then the judge left his chambers, and the Spencers filed out single file, Rob first and Eliza last. At the door Eliza turned and spoke to Mr. McCoy. "Miss Braddie, Marse Edward, the chillen an' I thank you kindly, sir. Not a cent of your money will be wasted."

Mr. McCoy raised his hand and nodded a yes-I-know nod, which made her duck her head from shyness. The family left the court house and walked down Baltimore Street, all talking at once, Katharine skipping ahead. Instead of walking home to celebrate, they boarded a horsecar at Paca Street. Rob paid the fare, three cents times five people—a lot of money. Riding along, Coos asked Rob how come Mr. McCoy happened to be at the hearing. Rob didn't know for sure. He guessed as Mr. McCoy and their father were both newspaper writers, most likely they were friends.

"Not fifty-dollars-a-month friends," Coos said. "We'd have met him at the house if he'd been that close."

The others agreed, and Eliza said, "I know how come he was dere. De Good Lord sent him."

"Fiddlesticks," quipped Coos. "How could He?" And Eliza replied, "Who hang de sun in de sky? Who tell de tide when to come in an' go out? Who notify de geese when it time to fly south an' show dem de way? You bes' be respectful, else he fiddlestick you with a bolt a lightnin'."

"I repent," Coos said, hands held palm to palm.

"Dat more like it," Eliza told him. Then, tapping Katharine on the knee, she said, "Quit kickin' your feet 'fore you wear out your shoes." And turning to Emily, "Stop starin' at de woman 'cross de aisle. You want people to think you never been on a streetcar before?"

Emily giggled, covering her mouth with her hand, and Eliza smiled at her. Emily was so trusting and friendly, she was easy to smile at. Then, too, although she favored her father, she was the closest thing to being Miss Braddie. And another thing, right then Eliza said she would have smiled at the devil himself.

"Fifty dollars ev'ry month," she said aloud. "Um-umm! Dat mighty fine. Wish my sister, Viney, Mable, and dem had been dere to hear our benefactor say what he say. Dey be proud as we are."

"Eliza?"

"What is it, Master Rob?"

"I was wondering about selling the house and moving and all and where we'll move to."

"One thing at a time," Eliza said. "Pull de cord. It time for us to get off."

20

Mrs. Smyth's Boarding House

Rob told the mailman about Eliza's gallant speech at the court house, and by late afternoon, practically everybody in the neighborhood was talking about it. By Sunday afternoon, the entire congregation at Ascension Church knew the story down to the last cent of the fifty dollars a month. Mrs. Hill C. Smyth was no exception. When she heard the news, she pricked up her ears for she was a widow with four children of her own, a house on Fayette Street, and not enough money. She was also a keen businesswoman with vision.

By taking in the Spencers as "paying guests," she would solve their problem and her own. As Eliza's reputation for cooking was known to anyone who ever attended a Christmas bazaar at Ascension (what pies, cakes, rolls, and homemade bread!), and as she would be part of the Spencer deal, Mrs. Smyth's problem would be more than solved. Eliza in the kitchen would be a feather in her cap—and before her marriage she had been a milliner!

Mrs. Smyth lost no time. With the minister Reverend Campbell Fair acting as go-between, the move took place.

A Promise is to Keep

"The Good Lord knew what He was doin'," Eliza later told me. "One house sold out from under our feet to pay debts; another waitin' wid de door open. It was all meant to be."

After the move, 125 Harlem Avenue was full of young people, four Spencers and three Smyths. The oldest Smyth boy had already left home to earn a living selling something on the road, Eliza didn't remember what. Bessie Smyth was a tall, dignified, sensible girl a year or so older than Rob. The boy Frew was the same age as Coos and almost as funny. Helen, a few years older than Emily, was a short girl with a round face, curly brown hair, and freckles on her nose.

At first the Smyths were not enthusiastic about the idea of boarders. However, Eliza soon won them over. The first wedge of winning came about over Miss Helen's freckles. Eliza gave her the famous, secret Harrison-Freckle-Fader Recipe memorized by Eliza from Miss Emily Harrison's scrap book: Mix and let stand for a week a tablespoon of lemon juice, a pinch of Borax, and a bit of fine sugar. Apply to "blighted areas" night and morning.

Eliza won over the rest of the family at the dinner time. To her pride, nobody could resist her pot roast, carrots, whole potatoes, salad, hot rolls, and apple pie. She declared the way those young people ate put her in mind of a flock of chickens at throwing-out-corn time.

Twice during the first dinner, Eliza felt obliged to poke Emily in the back to make her watch her manners. "Oh, I'm sorry, Mrs. Smyth, I didn't realize you wanted more gravy. Pass the gravy, Rob. The gravy, not the rolls." Once Miss Katharine needed poking for gulping her milk. The poke was left over from Miss Em. She had trained Eliza not to speak while serving, so she had to poke.

On the way to the kitchen to refill the vegetable dishes, Eliza thought to herself that Miss Braddie and Marse Edward would be pleased with the new setting. Rosa and Mable and Tom would be pleased, too. Without them and their training, along with Miss Em's, she could not have run either the boarding house kitchen or be the boarding housekeeper.

Plump Mrs. Smyth, straight from Ireland, had a rich, lusty humor that was not wasted on Eliza. She gave orders like a Confederate general, some of which Eliza obeyed and some of which she ignored. Mrs. Smyth always wore a lace cap on top of her fast-graying, neatly-parted brown hair. Every now and then she put on airs for Eliza's benefit, claiming she was used to silk dresses, not gingham aprons.

It didn't take Mrs. Smyth long to find out she would never make any money on her boarders. How could she? Eliza cooked lavishly with butter, sliced meat thick, made hot bread every day along with dessert, and encouraged third helpings. At breakfast on Sunday, lace-edged corn slappers, dripping maple syrup and melted butter, took the prize.

With all the work Eliza had to do, she saw to it that she was never overworked. "Door mat deserve what it get," she claimed. Early in the game she "read de riot act" to the entire household. After that the boys kept the woodbox full, ashes emptied, and the steps swept and washed clean as a hound's tooth. The girls kept their own rooms clean, beds made, halls and stairways dusted, and the dishes wiped.

Days went by swiftly. On school nights the young

people studied their lessons around the dining room table, the lamps pulled over to the edge. Mrs. Smyth darned in the sitting room, and in the kitchen Eliza sewed on a crazy quilt she was making for Miss Emily's hope chest. Not that Miss Emily was engaged or even thinking about it yet. So far her interest was in art. She was forever drawing and painting. And all Miss Katharine could think about was music. "It a blessed good thin' dey held on to Miss Braddie's piano," Eliza said.

Weekends were busy. Friday night was choir rehearsal with whist and refreshments later at Mrs. Smyth's, Eliza serving. Saturday night The Shakespeare Club met in the front room: the Spencers, the Smyths, young Charles Hayden, who was studying to be a lawyer, and his sister Caroline, and several others from Ascension.

Eliza enjoyed The Shakespeare Club. "Put me in mind a Marse Bradford back at Clay's Hope an' Marse Edward, those high soundin' words do." Sitting in the kitchen doorway, her ear out in the hall, she listened to Rob reading aloud.

> "Trifles light as air
> Are to the jealous
> Confirmations strong
> As Holy Writ."

"Why don't you join 'em in de parlor, honey?" she asked Katharine, who was sitting with her in the kitchen. "Dey havin' a good time."

"I don't want to read and recite," Katharine answered. "I want to play the piano."

"An' so you will," Eliza told her. "Anybody determined, single-minded to do somethin' will do it. Listen, Miss Bessie recitin' now."

Mrs. Smyth's Boarding House

Down the hall floated,

> "How far that little candle
> Throws his beam
> So shines a good deed
> In a naughty world."

"Is the world naughty, Eliza?" asked Katharine, her eyes round as a full moon. Eliza, stitching away, answered, "I recollect Miss Braddie say . . . now how it go? 'Nowhere anythin' kin be amiss when simpleness an' duty tend it.'" She rested her hands on top of her sewing, tears dimming her eyes, as she said: "I recollect somethin' else she used to say. It go dis a way:

> 'How poor are dey dat have not
>   patience
> What wound did ever heal but by
>   degrees.'"

"Did she make it up, Eliza?"
"Her or Marse Edward or Mr. Shakespeare. One, but I forget which."

And so the years went by: school, choir, club, skating on the lake at Druid Hill Park in winter (how Miss Em'ly could skate, skirt sailing, hands in her muff), and picnics in summer.

Regularly, the first day of every month, Mr. McCoy's fifty dollars arrived. Twice a week Mrs. Smyth went to market and brought back two large basketfuls of meat, fruit, and vegetables for Eliza to cook. A hundred times a day, seven days a week, Eliza walked back and forth across the boarding house kitchen floor: stove to table,

147

table to sink, sink to stove, and back to table. Sometimes she sang in her high, high voice, "Put John on the Island when the bride groom comes," the old song she sang back in still happier days.

Eliza never took a holiday, not even for a day. She claimed treading the earth in Miss Braddie's stead was a full-time job.

Even working all the time, she came up against a stone wall she couldn't climb over, so she said. No matter how hard she tried to save, she couldn't eke out of the money enough for piano lessons for Miss Katharine and Princeton for the boys. And Miss Katharine wanted to take piano lessons so much, and Marse Edward had his heart set on Princeton for his sons.

Never mind. Marse Edward and Miss Braddie would be proud of the way their children were turning out. After graduating from City College, Rob and Coos found jobs. They brought home enough money for the family to live on without Mr. McCoy's help. Eliza was mighty proud to send that news to Mr. McCoy, to tell him that they could manage from now on with Rob sweeping out the Pennsylvania Station and Coos in charge of a paper route with three boys working for him.

Emily graduated from Western High School, then earned her teacher's certificate and became a teacher. Sixteen years old she was then, Eliza told me, and she taught sixty-five first graders to read. Besides that, she taught the children to draw and paint and by doing so became a pioneer art teacher.

The Smyth girls became teachers also, Miss Bessie a principal in time, and a good one, so Eliza said. Miss

Mrs. Smyth's Boarding House

Katharine took piano lessons free from a neighbor and eventually won a scholarship to the Peabody Conservatory of Music. "She bound to," Eliza said. "Like I told her, she bound to win out."

Many changes had taken place outside 125 Fayette Street. Wounds of the war were healing slowly. Factories built in the North were booming. In the South fields were green again with corn, wheat, cotton, and tobacco. Many people were poor, though, both white and black. To exploit them, shrewd "carpetbaggers," men with money and an eye and nose for the quick dollar, bought up land, banks, and businesses to the detriment of the seller—usually, though not always.

Andrew Johnson, Lincoln's Vice President and after Lincoln's death, President, was impeached but not convicted. He was followed in office by U. S. Grant who in turn was followed by Garfield, who was shot. Eliza never knew why Mr. Garfield was shot. "Everybody know all about Mr. Lincoln, an' Mr. Garfield jes' as dead," she told Emily. "How come two presidents murdered in peace time? Down home where Miss Braddie an' I come from, a man who shoot a sittin' duck not worth greetin' on Sunday."

There were other important changes in the country. Bonnets were out, hats in, and dresses were pulled to the back with cascades to emphasize the pull. Some streetcars ran by electricity, though horsecars still ran on a great many lines. Wealthy people had electric lights in their homes and indoor plumbing.

"People remained de same, though, more or less," Eliza declared. "De good stayed good, de bad got worse. Southerners stayed Southerners. Northerners stayed Northerners. Some of both were cranky, some easygoing."

Eliza accepted most of the new-fangled ways and things as they came along. She balked at hats, though. "A bonnet tied on make a whole lot more sense than a pie pan perched on top a your head like a cock's comb," she told Miss Emily. Miss Emily liked pie pans, jabots, ruffles, bustles, flounces, and high button shoes with slightly pointed toes.

In many ways Emily and Eliza were alike. Both were small-boned, short, and too unselfish for their own good. Both lived every day to the hilt. On one subject they locked horns—Mr. Charles Hayden. When Miss Emily announced that she was going to marry "Charles" Eliza said, "Wid de whole world to choose from, how come you pick out a Yankee?" To which Miss Emily replied, "Oh Eliza, the Civil War has been over for ages. We are all Americans now."

Eliza raised her eyebrows skeptically. "What war got to do wid it? Duck in a chicken yard still a duck."

Duck and chicken, on August 31, 1893, Miss Emily Harrison Spencer and Mr. Charles S. Hayden were married at Ascension Church, The Reverend Campbell Fair officiating. Eliza knew Mr. Charley. She couldn't help knowing him for he and his sister Caroline were members of the choir, members of The Shakespeare Club, and in and out of the house for years. She couldn't help knowing him. He was a lawyer, a new one, smart, honorable to the bone, and handsome. Miss Emily adored his light, curly hair and hazel eyes and overlooked the fact that he was a Yankee. Completely overlooked it.

After the wedding, the bride and groom and Eliza

were at home in the new house on Mosher Street. Eliza had to go along with Miss Em'ly, she "natural-born had to," she said, "Miss Em'ly being Miss Braddie's oldest daughter." Anyway, Master Rob, Master Coos, and Miss Katharine could get along fine on their own, grown-up as they were by then. Besides, Miss Em'ly was so wrapped up in art and Mr. Charley, she needed Eliza to help keep house.

So a new era began, the next to last era for Eliza, the last being eternity.

21

Next to Last Era

Eliza's next to last era was in three parts: the years on Mosher Street, the years at the house on Windermere Avenue, and the years at Nancy's Fancy, Catonsville.

Before my sisters Ruth and Catherine and I came upon the scene, a word or two about Mr. Charley. Eliza declared that, smart as he was, he never did understand how she felt about money, how as a member of the family she couldn't take money from his hand. She said he tried to understand, but being a Yankee he couldn't. To settle the question to his satisfaction, he put money in the bank for her and now and then sent a check to Mable down at St. Michaels. Mable was very old by that time, nearly a hundred, and Tom and Rosa had been walking the golden streets for years.

Mr. Charley, Eliza told me, Yankee notwithstanding, measured up to her standards in a couple of ways. To begin with, every thing he planted in the ground grew. Then, too, he knew the stars by name and what they were doing up in the sky. Most important, he was a big help to Miss Em'ly and her art work. During the first year of their marriage, he took her all over the state so she could paint pictures in water colors of the Maryland wildflowers where they grew. During the same year he bought her a camera, taught her to take pictures, and taught her how to develop the plates and print the photographs in the sun out the back window.

During weekends that same year, he designed and built furniture in the cellar. According to Eliza, he finished the walnut crib in the nick of time.

On January 25, 1895 (cold as poverty it was that day, snow so deep the doctor had to climb through the second story window), Ruth, Miss Em'ly's first child, was born, and Eliza became Mammy all over again. From all reports, Ruth was a marvelous baby—solid dynamite from the start. "No sign a her dying, praise de Lord," Eliza said, her mind and heart flying back to Miss Braddie's dead babies. Miss Ruth had black eyes, not like Miss Braddie's or Miss Em'ly's or Marse Edward's. They were her own and they flashed lightning when Eliza didn't rock fast enough to suit her, or when she stopped singing too soon. It didn't take Ruth long to slide off of Eliza's lap, and from then on, try to catch her!

When Ruth was two years old, the family moved to a larger house on the corner of Windermere Avenue and Tinges Lane in Waverly, on the outskirts of Baltimore. Eliza liked the new house. It had a low front porch, safe for Ruth to play on with her friends. It also had ceiling to floor windows that let in a lot of sunlight and set off Miss Em'ly's lace curtains. Best of all was the backyard with a pump in the middle and at the far end a chicken house full of chickens. Eliza made a pet of a bantam hen, taught her to come in the kitchen, and lay an egg on a cushion under the kitchen table.

A Promise is to Keep

When Ruth was seven years old, a new baby was born, another girl, Catherine Spencer Hayden. The children were an appreciative and insatiable audience for Eliza's full repertoire—Tyson's Bull, The Buzzards, Lost My Needle, and all the rest. Catherine, the image of her father, was peace itself to Eliza after stormy Ruth. When Catherine was two years old Miss Em'ly's third and last child was born, another girl, Anna Bradford, named for both grandmothers, Nan for short. Me.

As far as my own memory goes, my first year is a total loss. However, from Mother's photographs, the time was well-spent. One picture is of me lying on Eliza's lap. Others are of Eliza holding me up—front view, side view, back view—me wearing a cap and long dress ready to go out, me undressed ready for the tub. In some of the pictures Ruth looks on. In others Catherine looks on. In a few pictures both sisters look on.

Most of the photographs taken that year are of Catherine because she was Botticelli-beautiful, with enormous brown eyes and light, curly hair. One picture, a prize winner and the one used on the cover of this book in its first printing, is of Ruth when she was five or six years old with her arms around Eliza's neck, both of them smiling as though nothing could be better.

When I was one year old, we moved to Nancy's Fancy, Catonsville, where Mother took pictures right and left: of the big old gray clapboard house, of the barn, of the tree by the spring, of the little stone house—from all sides and in all seasons. The catalpa tree by the front porch often posed and so did the gnarled pear tree at the side gate.

Next to Last Era

Only a few photographs were taken inside the house because flashbulbs had not been invented. However, I need no pictures to remind me of everything including my young self. I see myself hop off my bicycle, burst into the house, fling my school books on the hall table and yell, "Mother, Eliza, I'm home."

Instantly the quiet house springs to life. Mother, standing in the living room doorway, book in hand, says, "You must be starving. Get something to eat, then come tell me everything that happened today."

I see myself run down the dark hall, through the sunny dining room to the marvelous-smelling kitchen to Eliza and to something to eat.

Eliza's room was on the second floor at the end of the hall between the bathroom, where Mother developed her photographic plates, and the corner room, where she spread out her wet prints to dry on a sheet spread on the floor.

We did not go into Eliza's room uninvited, and invited we went in respectfully. The wooden bed was always neat as pie—the center puffed up like a muffin. A quilt made by Eliza was always folded at the foot.

Mother's room down the hall had an open fireplace with a coal grate for winter. On real cold nights Eliza would bring a hot flat iron up from the kitchen and iron our bed warm down where our bare feet would be. Catherine and I slept together in the white iron bed with brass knobs.

One of Mother's pictures is of Catherine sitting up in the bed, her arm around her knees and her long curls tied back with a ribbon. Another picture is of me dressed in a white nightgown looking for Santa Claus out Ruth's window.

A Promise is to Keep

Ruth's room was up front—up five steps from the landing, so my feet remember. My feet also remember my earliest image of Eliza. I was four, or nearly four, and I'd gotten my feet wet outdoors. Eliza sat me on a kitchen chair, took off my damp shoes and stockings, and put on dry things. I can still feel my feet resting in her comfortable lap. She gave me a feeling of security, home, all things good. Another memory lives in the first finger of my left hand. I'd gotten a splinter in it from the sliding board. Out of the kitchen cupboard Eliza got her basket full of everything anybody needed to live. With a needle she took out the splinter. Then to my pride and joy she made me a finger stall, sewed it to fit, slipped it over the finger, tied it around my wrist, then said, "Away she goes."

Back to photographs again. Eliza was the prime poser for the mile-high stack of pictures. She is always wearing a white head handkerchief, "To keep the thousand legs from crawling in my ears," she explains. Pictures show her making jelly, sewing, making bread, greeting the mailman, stuffing the Thanksgiving turkey. In one picture she is patting oysters for Uncle Robbie, who was at our house on a visit from Pittsburgh. His pants are not too short now, his sleeves not too short, and his toes don't bump against the toes of his shoes.

In another picture Eliza is making beef hash for Miss Katharine, who by that time was Mrs. Gellert Alleman, wife of Dr. Gellert Alleman, chemistry professor at Swarthmore College. To Eliza's chagrin, Dr. Alleman was a Yankee and German to boot.

We didn't see much of Uncle Lindsly—Eliza's Coos. He had a farm of his own near Sykesville, Maryland, and wild horses couldn't drag him away from it. Once in a while his sons Edward and Lindsly spent the day with us to race around the lawn, jump out of the hay loft into a pile of hay, play high-spy and prisoner's base, and eat huge lunches cooked by Eliza. I never did know whether their mother, Aunt Lila, was a "foreigner" or not. As Eliza didn't mention it, I presume she was not. Aunt Marion, Uncle Rob's wife, was. She came from Pittsburgh.

What a grand time we had now that it was our turn to hear Eliza's songs, poems and stories, to play her games, to get to know all about Clay's Hope, Mount Pleasant, The Martin's Nest, and to meet Marse Bradford, Tom, Mable, Rosa, Viney, and the rest of Eliza's family and, of course, Miss Braddie and Marse Edward.

Could anybody be as noble and full of fun as Miss Braddie as pictured by Eliza? Perhaps not. Then again, maybe so. After all, Eliza was just the way I picture her: sure, strong, courageous, and joyful.

If only she could have died at home with us. She died alone in a hospital on May 14, 1921 when she was eighty-five years old. No, not alone. The Lord was with her. He promised to be, and a promise is to keep, so Eliza said.

The promise I made to her was kept. My parents saw to that. Eliza Ann Benson is buried where she wanted to be: next to Miss Braddie in the Spencer family graveyard.

Epilogue

During the summer of 1983, my nephew Sidney Wanzer and his wife, Anne (Yankees form Concord, Massachusetts) came down to snoop around Maryland with me. The three of us wandered around the Eastern Shore, visiting places where Eliza and Braddie were born and grew up. We also paid our respects to the graves of Sister Em and Cousin Willie alongside Christ Episcopal Church at St. Michaels. From there we went on to visit other family graves at Spencer Hall, Solitude, and Crooked Intention. We tried to find Braddie's mother's grave at Kirkum but were defeated by brambles, overgrown bushes, wet grass, and stick-me-tights.

Enough about graves and on to The Martin's Nest. Remember The Martin's Nest—the farm near Randallstown—where Edward Spencer's parents lived, where Edward and his brother were born, where Edward, Braddie, and Eliza lived for years after the wedding?

Before my husband John died, he and I tried half-heartedly to find the farm. I say half-heartedly because we didn't really want to find it, both of us predicting that progress had knocked down the house and cut the land into checkerboard lots.

Epilogue

Sidney, determined to find the farm no matter what, studied a 1968 reprint of the 1877 Atlas of Baltimore County that had been in my bookcase for ages. On page 8, Second District, Randallstown, he saw a dot off in an open field on the left, E. Spencer written beside it in minute letters.

"That's it," he said, tapping the dot. "That's The Martin's Nest."

I'd seen the dot before, said so, and added, "Most likely by now nothing is left of anything."

Ignoring my remark, Sidney telephoned the Baltimore County Court House. After a long conversation, a longer wait, and still another long conversation during which he took notes, he hung up the receiver and told Anne and me, "We cross town, take the Liberty Road to Randallstown, turn left on Offut Road, go as far as Brice's Run, on for a mile or two until we come to a driveway with white stone gateposts, and that's it."

We followed the directions and finally came to what could be Brice's Run. It was a lively creek hurrying on its way with purpose, murmuring to itself happily. But was it Brice's Run?

To be sure, we decided to ask somebody. As nobody came along the road, we turned in a most unfriendly driveway with threats nailed on trees—"Private Property—Keep Out," "No Trespassing," and "Intruders Going Beyond This Point Will Be Shot."

Sidney stopped the car, maneuvered it around, and we left feeling a bit discouraged. We didn't stay discouraged, though, for a mile and a half down the main road we came to the two white gateposts on the left. So the creek we passed over was Brice's Run, and we'd found what we were looking for.

A Promise is to Keep

We drove in and down a threatless driveway. The farmhouse was a low, two-story building with an appealing swoop to the roof, two red brick chimneys— one slimmer than the other, porch across the front, and flowers blooming in front of the porch. A perfect setting. "Pretty as a han' paintin'," Eliza would say. Green fields, an orchard with lovely old trees, and down the hill sat a big old barn four times the size of the house.

"This is it," Sidney said with conviction, and Anne and I agreed.

Nobody was home except two cats, who chose to remain aloof. Never mind, the place itself was there. "Yes indeedy." The Martin's Nest was there, peaceful, beautiful, and quiet except for bees humming and a cricket sounding off in the orchard.

A light breeze blew over me. Tingling, I felt kin to everything around me—the earth, the trees, the house, the barn. Nothing seemed new to me—and yet it was.

"Yes indeedy." No doubt about that.